GENIUS GENUINE

Samuel Chifney

General Books

www.General-Books.net

Publication Data:

Title: Genius Genuine
Author: Chifney, Samuel, Ca. 1753-1807
Reprinted: 2010, General Books, Memphis, Tennessee, USA
Publisher: London : sold for the author
Publication date: 1804
Subjects: George IV, King of Great Britain, 1762-1830
Horses
Horse-racing – Great Britain
Horses – Training

How We Made This Book for You
We made this book exclusively for you using patented Print on Demand technology.
First we scanned the original rare book using a robot which automatically flipped and photographed each page.
We automated the typing, proof reading and design of this book using Optical Character Recognition (OCR) software on the scanned copy. That let us keep your cost as low as possible.
If a book is very old, worn and the type is faded, this can result in numerous typos or missing text. This is also why our books don't have illustrations; the OCR software can't distinguish between an illustration and a smudge.
We understand how annoying typos, missing text or illustrations, foot notes in the text or an index that doesn't work, can be. That's why we provide a free digital copy of most books exactly as they were originally published. You can also use this PDF edition to read the book on the go. Simply go to our website (www.general-books.net) to check availability. And we provide a free trial membership in our book club so you can get free copies of other editions or related books.
OCR is not a perfect solution but we feel it's more important to make books available for a low price than not at all. So we warn readers on our website and in the descriptions we provide to book sellers that our books don't have illustrations and may have numerous typos or missing text. We also provide excerpts from each book to book sellers and on our website so you can preview the quality of the book before buying it.
If you would prefer that we manually type, proof read and design your book so that it's perfect, simply contact us for the cost. We would be happy to do as much work as you would be like to pay for.

Limit of Liability/Disclaimer of Warranty:
The publisher and author make no representations or warranties with respect to the accuracy or completeness of the book. The advice and strategies in the book may not be suitable for your situation. You should consult with a professional where appropriate. The publisher is not liable for any damages resulting from the book.
Please keep in mind that the book was written long ago; the information is not current. Furthermore, there may be typos, missing text or illustration and explained above.

GENIUS GENUINE

1

GENIUS GENUINE

The Prince's Question to Chifney Page 94
    The Prince and Sir Charles Bunbury on the subject of Escape 97
    The Stewards of the Jockey-Club examine Chifney 99
    Sir Charles Bunbury telling the Prince of Wales no Gentleman would start against him 112
    References to some recent Facts, as furnishing positive Proofs tliat the Misrepresentations of my Conduct in riding Escape on the 21st of October 1791 slill operate cruelly against me; and rendering indispensable the publication of my Narrative.114
    Mr. Cookson taking Chifney off his horse Sir Harry, at York, c Il7
    Affidavit on Escape's running 137
    To those not well acquainted with the Turf respecting Horses Changing in their Running 141
    CONTENTS. Vll
    Mr. W. Lake and Neale telling the Prince Chifney had lost on His Royal Highness's Horse Fitzwilliam Page 14g
    Duke of Bedford taking Chifney off his Horses 152
    Duke of Bedford taking Chifney off his

Horse Fidget 154
Paul and Augusta run twice on the same day 155
Riding with a loose rein 157
Reasons why the Turf Horses degenerate, and Guides to recover them to their Strength and Speed 163

ABUSES
THAT ARE GONE ABROAD.

I AM repeatedly told, by respectable people and from all quarters, that it is talked in their counties that Chifney lost intentionally upon His Royal Highness the Prince of Wales's horse Escape, at Newmarket, on the 20th of October 1791; and after Escape had pulled up on this said race to walk back to scale, that Chifney was laughing to the Prince of Wales because he had got Escape beat; and then, to suit their wicked construction, they said, and I find that it is sent out to the world, that the Prince won such an immense sum of money upon Escape the following day; and that the Prince gives Chifney two hundred guineas a year for his life after l)is losing this said race with Escape.

SAMUEL CHIFNEYS REASONS

THIS PUBLICATION, I AM fully aware of the singularity and auk-wardness of the circumstances under which I am forced to appear before the public upon paper.

I do not conceive that any noblemen or gentlemen whom I have the honour of addressing, can be ignorant of the sensation that was made on the turf when I had the honour of riding His Royal Highness the Prince of Wales's Horse Escape, at Newmarket, on the 20th and 21st days of October 1791- Some may say this is an old story, and long since forgotten, and that I am wrong to revive it.

I have but one answer to make to all such observations; which is, that I have felt the effects of the occurrences of those days have operated B 2 upon upon me in the most severe manner, after a lapse of many years. I presume then, that the liberality of my readers will admit that I have a right to be indig-nant at the gross mis-statements of my riding Escape on the 20th October 1791, which imposed upon me appearing on paper before the public, as the only means I possess of doing justice, with an exposition of the truth, to those who have been beguiled into errors. This it will be impossible to do without mentioning the names of persons who happened to be actors in the scenes which I relate.

I claim the universal right of self defence; and shall be strictly observant of the most scrupulous veracity, as I mean to annex hereto an affidavit of the truth which in the course of the narrative I shall assert.

Now in my self defence, I think it necessary for me to begin by stating some of Mr. Warwick Lake's conduct, as I think that will clearly shew how capable he was of using that sort of severity to the Prince of Wales, which coupled coupled the Prince with Chifncy's running Escape a cheat, (seen in page 86,) and before I was engaged to the Prince, Mr. Vernon's servant (James Edwards,) told me, that both Messrs. Warwick Lake and Neale had said, that Chifney should not come to live with the Prince, and if he did, he should not stay. However, on the 14th of July 1790, His Royal Highness the Prince of Wales did me the honour to engage me for life to ride his running horses, at a salary of two hundred guineas a year. At this time Mr. W. Lake had the management of His Royal Highness's ruiming horses, to match, bet, c.

Soon after I had been engaged, His Royal Highness told me, " if at any time it should happen ' that I give you orders how to ride, you will al-" ways go to Mr. Warwick Lake to finish your " orders, and Mr. Lake and you will make any " alteration you like, and run as you please."

When at Lewes, on the 7 th of August 179O, I was going to ride Scota for the Ladies' plate, four miles, against Lord Barrymore's Highlander and

Mr. Clarke's Schoolboy, His Royal Highness came to me and sdid " Sam Chifncy, I shall be very glad to see you win upon Scota to-day, for ' she is never to run again whether she win or " lose. Go to Mr. W. Lake for your orders how to ride her."

When I went to Mr. W. Lake, he gave me orders to make very strong running with Scota, for she was the slowest mare that ever ran, but the stoutest. I told Mr. Lake I knew her to be neither. He replied, I knew nothing about her, for she was quite a different mare in her trials; that she was sure of winning, run which way she would; but he strictly enjoined me to make very strong running with her. I then told Mr. W. Lake I thought she could not win, run which way she would; but to run her as he ordered would be the most certain way to beat her. I urged Mr. Lake to allow me to use gentle means with her, provided other horses make tolerable good running, but could not prevail upon him to alter his first orders; at which I was much distressed.

tressed, lest my conduct should suffer with the public for riding Scota in the way I was ordered; and if so, I thought I might suffer with His Royal Highness, thinking that Mr. Lake would not satisfy them that it was his order for Scota to run in this sort of way. It being now saddling time, I had no opportunity to go to His Royal Highness; I accordingly made up my mind to wait with Scota, and abide the consequence, meaning to tell His Royal Highness, after the race, that I was afraid to ride Scota according to Mr. Lake's orders: but as Scota won, I did not like to trouble His Royal Highness on the subject. I had seen Scota run most or all her races; I had rode her for Colonel OKelly; I knew her to be a fast runner and a very great jade, four miles, if strong running were made; and the field I believe knew she was fast and a jade. I waited with Scota, and Highlander and Schoolboy waited behind her, till, I think, within 150 yards of the winning-post. I then thought Scota, if she got the first effort, would nt)ulcl live in a sharp rally. T tried it, and she just won a very hard race. I think Scota must have been beat a very great way if strong running play had been made; I think such as two hundred yards, as she was not in condition for running. I had just come out of the scale when Mr. Charles Davies, the bettor, gave me joy upon v. inning so unexpectedly. I denied having won unexpectedly. Mr. Davies persisted in it that I had won unexpectedly. Conscious as I was of having communicated my opinion to none but Mr. W. Lake, I asked Mr. Davies what was his motive for saying that I had won unexpectedly. Mr. Davies then assured me that Mr. Lake had betted with him against Scota, and had afterwards advised him to edge his money off, for Scota could win no way. On the 20th of October 179O Magpie ran with Lord Barrymore's Seagull and others for a handicap sweepstakes, and in this race Seagull gave Magpie eight pounds, and Magpie beat Seagull several lengths. I took the first opportunity, after this race, of recommending to His Royal

Highness

Highness to match Magpie with Seagull, at iiinii stone each, to run the same course, on the next day, for two liundred guineas, observing that I had rather run at even than that Magpie should receive weight but at nine stone. I then suggested to His Royal Highness that I thought the odds would be upon Seagull, as Seagull stood very high in the public opinion. I therefore recommended to His Royal Highness to lay out five or six hundred more before starting, as the market for betting was; and, with leave, I would bet His Royal Highness fifty guineas upon Magpie.

On the next morning His Royal Highness sent for me, and told me, in the presence of Mr. Lake, that Mr. Lake could not match Magpie against Seagull last night; and observed, "You know, Sam Chifney, we cannot always match as we " wish." I expressed my humble satisfaction, and said, that had they chosen to have run I should have liked the match.

His Royal Highness then said that Mr. Lake would try again that night to match them; and c I took took the liberty of replying, that if they were not matched on that night to run the next day, should decline having any thing to do with the matching them.

On this same niglit Mr. Lake matched them to riln tlie same course on the 2d of November 79 Seagull was to give Magpie eight pounds, but Magpie was not to carry more than eight stone; and on the morning of the race His Royal Highness sent forme into his room, and asked mc if Magpie would win that day. I answered that I did not think he would. His Royal Highness then replied, You don't think he will! Why what does this mean, Sam Chifney? This is your own match!" I then said, "Yes, " your Royal Highness, it is my own match, and I am veiy thankful to your Royal tlighness for " indulging me; but I dont know that Magpie ' is well, which is the reason why I don't think he will win." His Royal Highness observed

My match was done away by not being made to my time, that I answered too free.

that 19 that Frank Neale (the training groom) had just quitted the room before I entered it, and had assured him that Magpie was as fit to run as aiiy horse could be. I then took the Hberty and told His Royal Highneas that if Magpie was well to Tun, he was as sure of winning as ever horse was; and notwithstanding Neale's saying the horse was well to run, I wished Ilis Royal Highness not to lose more upon him than the match-money.

When I saw Magpie stripped for saddling, I knew him exceedingly unfit to run, (but whether this was from the ignorance or rascality of Neale, I know not,) and he was beaten with extraordi-nary ease, I thought. He could not go a running pace in any part of the race. After I had come out of the scale I rode to the side of the betting-ring, where Mr. W. Lake observed to me how easily Magpie had been beaten. I then told Mr. Lake that I should have been glad if he had tried him, as he sometimes ran 150 or 200 yards better at one time than at another; and Mr, Lake directly replied that Frank Neale had c l informed 20 inibrmed liini that Magpie had bad Icgs that he dared not gallop liim. I think Neale should be heard on this saying of Mr. W. Lake's, that he dared not gallop Magpie, his having bad legs.

This was the last time of Magpie's running, and Ije was turned out of training after this raee, but for what reason I never knew. I knew nothing about his legs being amiss;

I saw nothing amiss in them before starting; but I did observe that his condition was such as must stop his legs from going as they ought. I believe that Mag–T)ie, had he been fit to run, was the best runner of his age then on the turf. Seagull was the same age as Magpie.

When I recommended the match between Magpie and Seagull to be run on the 21st of October, at nine stone each, I had a particular reason for fixing the day for running; and those very reasons made me unwilling to match them at any future time.

Mr. Lake matching to run on the 2d of November, this, with what I had before observed of

Mr. W. Lake's conduct, impressed my mind strongly; for, as Magpie had just beaten Seagull at the same weight, and with great ease, I could not see how Mr. W. Lake could be able to have eight pounds given him to run the same course again. I viewed this eight pounds as a strong lure for me; for if His Royal Highness backed Magpie, it was likely to afford plenty of customers, at a different price, in betting. These thoughts made me pay very strict attention to Magpie's management; and from my observation of it I judged that he was likely to be very unfit to run; but of this I could not be positively certain till I saw him stripped for saddling, for I did not go into His Royal Highness's stable at Newmarket but once, I think, when I attended His Royal Highness there for a few minutes.

I find it requisite to mark one other instance of the singularity of Mr. W. Lake's conduct. A match had been made for Traveller to run on the 6th of November 17 90, against Lord Barrymore's Highlander. Highlander was seven years old, and

Traveller 22 Traveller only five. Traveller gave Highlander fifteen pounds four miles for five hundred guineas. Before this match was to be run. Traveller was tried the same length and course and weight that he had to run with Highlander.

He was tried with Phalanx, Bubble, and Archibald. When they had about half a mile to run, the other horses were so very much beaten by Phalanx that (Mr. W. Lake and Neale, who from the rising ground on our right commanded every horse's situation) I called to know if we might give over running, and they said, yes: at which time Phalanx was more than ten lengths before Bubble, Bubble was many lengths before Traveller, and Traveller was about his own length before Archibald; so that it was hurting the horses to distress them after Phalanx any longer.

On the morning Traveller and Highlander were to run. His Royal Highness sent for me, and Mr. W. Lake was in his room. His Royal Highness said, "Sam Chifney, will Traveller win to- day?" I replied, "No, your Royal Highness, I

"don't don't think he will." Mr. W. Lake directly said, "Why don't you think he will? You know " he ran a good horse in his trial, for you rode " him." I answered, "Yes, Sir, I rode him, " but I don't know that he ran a good horse. Mr. Lake then replied with much warmth, "Yes, " you do know that he ran a good horse, for he " was not beaten more than half a lengthhe " was not beaten a length." I replied with astonishment, "Not a length. Sir!"" No!" said Mr. Lake, " he was beaten very little more than a lengthhe was not beaten a length and a " half."

Mr. W. Lake now clearly shewed to me a wish to disguise the truth, and spoke with such warmth that I thought His Royal Highness appeared much disturbed. I therefore thought it most proper for me to bow and quit the room, which I did, thinking to have an opportunity of informing His Royal Highness, before I rode Traveller, how he ran on his trial. When upon the course I saw His Royal Highness on horseback.

back, I took the liberty of thus addressing hrm, "With leave from your Royal Highness I shall " be glad to name how Traveller ran on his trial." His Royal Highness said, ' You may name."

I then related to His Royal Highness the trial Traveller ran, and was beaten with extraordinary ease. He ran worse in this match, I think, than, he had done on his trial, for he appeared to me notable to go a proper running pace in any part of the race. My cautious manner in answering Mr. W. Lake, when I said I did not know that Traveller had run a good horse, was because I knew none of the horses' weights they were tried with but the horse Traveller that I rode.

Of some Occurrences at the Spring Meeting at Neiimarhct in 1791

On the I2th of May 1791, Mr. W. Lake gave me orders to make play with Pegasus against Car-clock and another horse for the King's Plate. His Royal Highness not being at Newmarket, I used my utmost endeavours to induce Mr. Lake to allow me to wait with Pegasus: he would not agree to it; however, as I knew Pegasus's making play was the only way to beat him, I took upon myself to wait with him, and he just won. Had Pegasus made play, I believe Cardock would have beaten him. Pegasus was very unfit to run in this race, though a much better runner at that time than Cardock.

From the Prince telling me, in page 13, for Mr. Lakeanj me to run as we pleased, was giving me some toleration occasionally in my running.

D Some 26 Some little time after this race was over, Mr. W. Lake came up to me, and said, "I give " you joy, Chifney; I was glad to see the horse " win; T mean, I was glad for the horse's master's " sake, fori don't mind any thing about them for myself." This I thought was strange talk. I observed, however, to Mr. Lake, that Pegasus was nearly being beaten, from being very unfit to run: and I further remarked that it was ridiculous for His Royal Highness's horses to be so very often brought o t unfit to run, without any account being given for it. I told Mr. W. Lake that Neale was unqualified to act as groom to His Royal Highness. I was particularly disgusted with the assurance with whjch Neale supported his ignorance. I hkt-wise told Mr. W. Lake that he was the most in fault to sufter those goings on. I did not recommend abuse to Neale, and told Mr. Lake that Neale wanted assistance. I knew, where there were so many horses continually running, that tlierf must be many changes in their running; but it is the groom's place to account to his master nearly tlie cause of those changes; for by his accounting to his master, it is Hkcly then to be accounted for to the public, which is fair; because much of the public back their opinions on horses, imagining the groom to be a person of ability and integrity where they are in such very high office.

D 2 JVhat IVkat happened at York Races in 1791 I WAS ordered down to York to ride Traveller and Creeper, and I understand that many of the turf people have given out that on the first day of the races I rode Traveller a cheat to match him, c. There needs no other reason for my entering into a detail of what occurred on the occasion. I arrived at York on the Saturday preceding the races, and saw Mr. Casborne the groom, and inquired of him how the horses were: he assured me they were both well, and asked me if I wished to see them. I answered, yes, as I meant to send to His Royal Highness that night. He first shewed me Traveller, and I directly observed that he was not fit to run, and that I should report him so to His Royal Highness that niglit. I added, that I was sorry for it, and particularly ticulany so on liis account. Casbonic now-questioned me particularly vhy Traveller was not well to run, and I informed him, at wliieh he appeared to be very sorry. He then conducted mc into the other stable to see Creeper, and 1 told him that I was very glad to see Creeper look so well, iind that I should say as much to His Royal Highness that night. I was always glad to have Cas-borne with the horses, as I thought liim more careful, and that he knew better how to train. This opinion of mine, I believe, was known to His Royal Highness. I sent to inform His Royal Highness that Traveller was not well to run, and that Creeper was well to run, and I wished His Royal Highness would back Creeper in London. On Monday the 22d of August Ijg Traveller ran with Spadille, Gustavus, and Fox, and after he had run about two miles and a quarter he stopped very short. I foiloved the horses with him as well as I was able; but they leaving him at such a very great distance, I thought it prudent to pull him up; and I now thought Traveller good

C, oodibr nothing for running, as he was beat such a wonderful way.

I was told Mr. W. Lake did not come on the jxround till after Traveller's race; and when the day's sport was over, I asked him leave to run Creepcr-and Traveller together the next morning. 1 told him why I wislied to run them. I added that I did not wish to run them with any view of learning Creeper's goodness: that could not be; as Traveller's running was so very much gone from him, that there was no weight that could bring him up to run with any horse; neither could it be of the least injury to Creeper for his race on the next day. Accordingly on the next morning, which was the 23d of August 1791? I got on Creeper without weighing. I think I rode about 8st. gib. and a little boy rode Traveller, not more than 6st. 3lb. as Casborne had said Creeper was five, and Traveller six years old. At starting, I told the boy to go first with Traveller, I wi. hed Creeper to know the course, he was such a very long-stroking horse.

and let him go as well as he thought he was able, so as not to knock him up, for Traveller was a very free runner: and after he had run two miles as fast as he was very well able, I went up to him with Creeper, and told the boy to pull his horse and gallop him very gently the same way back. I then kept a great way behind him. In my opinion this running was much less fatigue to Creeper than the gallop he would or should have had this same morning if he had not run with Traveller: and this same morning, viz. the 23d of August 1791, I learned that Mr. W. Lake had matched Traveller, on the over-night, against Cavendish, to run in the Spring following, over Newmarket, for five hundred guineas; and on this same day, when I saw Mr. Lake I toid him I thought he was bold in matcliing Traveller at this time against any horse. Mr. Lake replied, "If the Prince don't like to stand the match, Ill stand every ' guinea of it myself." I then observed to Mr. Lake his motive for matching him probably was from his last trial at Newmarket, in the spring; 32 spring; to which he said, "Yes." I told Mr. W. Lake that he would not have matched him had he come in time to have seen him run, and I was afraid his running would never come to him again. Mr. Lake appeared displeased, and again repeated that if the Prince did not like to stand the match, he would stand every guinea of it himself. To which I replied, that if he made a good match, the Prince stood it, and if he made a had match the Piince did not want him to stand it.

On the following day, the 24th of August 1791, Creeper ran against Walnut, and the instant I had stripped Creeper for saddling, I believed him poisoned for the race, for his carcase was svvelled in so extraordinary a manner, that I never saw a horse so before, and I knew him to have been in fine order only the morning before.

Nothing could be now done for His Royal Highness, and I thought it better for me to lose all my money than to have any complaint made to His Royal Highness, that I made the horses wait wait for me at starting. Mr. W. Lake and Mr. Vauxhall Clark must sufter with mc for I dared not to go to the betting stand to tell them, and no person was at hand that I could send with such a message. Directly the horses started there was a very great change in Creeper's going; he could not get his legs out, which I attributed to the swelling of his carcase. It happened that there was but little running made till they came near home; and when they came near the grand stand. Walnut and Creeper had a run together; and Creeper had evidently the best of that run; and yet, notwithstanding the short distance in. Creeper was beaten three or four lengths.

I believe that Creeper must have been beaten a great way if there had been tolerable good mnmng made all the way. I lost upon Creeper, jn this race, two hundred guineas. I betted all this money with Mr. Lake and Mr. Vauxhall Clark. After Creeper was beaten by Walnut, it was said that I had lost the race by trying him; this I think is most likely to be sent out by those E that that knew of his having been poisoned for the race, and this I thought was done by him who had the care of the horse. On the following day, the 25th of August 1791, which was on Thursday, Traveller ran again against Tickle-Toby, Walnut, Gustavus, Cavendish, and Dubskelper; they ran the same course that Traveller ran on the preceding Monday; Tickle-Toby won; and Traveller was beaten in this race, to the best of my belief, part of Tickle-Toby's head only, notwithstanding Traveller being placed third. Mr. Belston, who lives at Leathcrhead, in Surrey, came to me before starting, and said, "Chifney, "I will give you twenty guineas if you will per-' suade Mr. Lake not to run Traveller, as he had got one hundred guineas Traveller against Walnut in their places, and that he had no " chance for it if Traveller started." I told Mr, Belton I wished he had not named about twenty

There was something very singular in Casbornei manner before me on the day before; but I had no thoughts of his doing any thing unfair to Creeper till I stripped him for saddling.

guineas.

guineas, neither could I be of any service to him about Traveller's not running; and why had he not gone to Mr. Lake? Mr. Belston said he had been to Mr. Lake, and he told him that Traveller must run. I told Mr. Belston that Mr. Lake had answered him very properly, for it was the Prince's pleasure to send his horses to York to run, and whether they could run well or not, they should run; and that I could only recollect, that his bet was in their pieces; and should any thing extraordinary occur so as to enable me to pass Walnut before he should get in, that I would take care to do it. Mr. Belston said he was much obliged to mc. A long distance from home Traveller had been much beat by Tickle-Toby and Walnut, and some lengths beiind them in the last one hunclrvd yards; but finding Traveller stayed to his running, and the horses before him slackening their pace, I continued pressing him very severe; and just before getting to the winning-post, Traveller poured upon them, and Walnut dropped to the hind part E 2 qf of Tickle-Toby, and Iickle-Toby stopped very short; but I thought part of his head passed the winning-post before Traveller's. The shout was, Traveller won! and a yard by the winning-post. I believe Traveller's head was clearly before Tickle-Toby's; that the people not even with the winning-post might easily be mistaken. When I got to scale, it was as I thought, Tickle-Toby won; and my giving Traveller great time to come back to scale, the other riders had weighed. I got into scale, and the man that weighed us said to me, "You weigh third." I said, "I was se- cond." The man immediately took me by the arm to pull me out of the scale, saying, "You " shall not weigh if you don't weigh third." I called to the gentlemen in the stand above the scales to know if Mr. Rhodes was there, thinking him the judge. When Mr. Rhodes appeared, I asked him who was second. When Mr. Rhodes spoke, he said Walnut; I now saw Traveller must be placed wrong. I said to the man, "You " will be pleased to weigh me, and it makes no

"difference diffcrence to me whether Traveller is placed second or third; but Traveller was second." Mangles, Walnut's rider, said, "No, Mr. Chif- ney. Walnut was second, he beat Traveller near " his length." When I asked Mr. Rhodes which was second, Mr. Rhodes appeared not desirous of speaking, and when he did speak, it was in a Jiushing manner. I had always a singular good opinion of Mr. Rhodes's punctuality. This was my very reason for not daring to go on the day before, at saddling time, to tell Mr. Lake and Mr. Clark I thought Creeper was poisoned for his race, as I thought Mr. Rhodes would not show partiality to any one in waiting above the time that he had given orders for saddling and starting, but to start and go without those that were not ready. Had I been at Newmarket I could have bought myself time to have gone to Mr. Lake and Mr. Clark, as the penalty there is five guineas if the training-groom or rider make the horses wait at starting. If Mr. Rhodes was not judge, he might speak after the judge, or the man at the scale. I was afterwards told that the man who weighed us was the judge, and that he was huntsman to the city hounds.

I asked Hindley, who rode Tickle-Toby, which horse that was that was by the side of him as he passed" the winning-post. Hindley said he did not know. I did not recollect at scale about Mr. Belston's bet, and glad I was, as it could only have served to aggravate me.

I had the same desire of winning upon Traveller, on the first day at York, as ever I had to win on any horse.

When this race was over, Mr. Baker's groom, Tyziman, seeing Traveller had beaten Cavendish a great way, he pressed me very much to let him and Thomas Fields, the rider, off of fifty guineas which they stood with their master, Mr. Baker, on Cavendish against Traveller, the match over Newmarket the spring following, which had been made on the Monday night.

Tickle-Toby and Traveller were so near to each other passing the winning-post, that Walnut was shut out by them.

Tyziman

Tyziman said he knew the match was all of my making, and that he was very sure that I could let him off the fifty guineas if I pleased.

I told Mr. Tyziman that I had nothing to do about Traveller and Cavendish being matched, neither could I be of any service to him in his bet- I do not know that I should have made Mr. Tyziman any answer, only before this I had much respect for him, as I did and do think him a good trainer. I had just marked him out with the intention of recommending him as a fit person for His Royal Highness's service as a training-groom; but after I found he knew more about me than I knew of myself, and seeing him capable of pressing to be off a fifty-guinea bet at a time which was so very unseasonable, I believed this sort of conduct of Mr. Tyziman's was not fit for a prince's servant. It was likewise said at Newmarket I rode Traveller a cheat the first day at York, to back him for the Thursday's race.

Of the Occurrences relative to Escape.

In order to give myself a fair and clear chance of being thoroughly understood in all that refers to Escape, I shall beg leave to disclose my earliest thoughts of him, from the first time he attracted my notice, which was at Newmarket in April 1789. I thougiit Escape lost against Harpator from his not waiting when they ran over the Duke's Course.

And in the next October Meeting, in 178(), Escape beat Nimble across the Flat (I thought) with extraordinary ease; and I considered Nim ble a fast runner. From this time I had a very-high opinion of Escape's speed.

I was not present at Ascot Heath races in June 1790, but if I be correctly informed how that race was run. Escape lost the Oatlands Stakes there from not waiting.

Ill the month of August 1790 I was ordered to York to ride Escape, and directly after my return, Mr. George Leigh, a person in His Royal High-ness's household, told me, on Egham race-ground, that my conduct about Escape, at York, had been much canvassed and blamed by the company at Wooburn, and by none so much as by the Duke of Queensberry. I shall therefore be particular in all that occurred on this occasion. Before I set out for York I had been informed that His Royal Highness had taken three thousand to two thousand, in one bet, that Escape won both the Great Subscriptions; and immediately upon my arrival there I asked Casborne if Escape were well to run. Ele answered, "Yes;" but upon my telling him my reasons why he was not so, Casborne came over to my opinion. I imputed no fault to Casborne, but thought he had not had Escape under his care a sufficient time to get him into running order. I charged Casborne, as he was most likely to see Mr. W. Lake first, in his way to York, to communicate these sentiments to him, which I would certainly do, the first time I should see him.

I no sooner saw Mr. W. Lake than I told him thatescape was not fit to run; yet I thought he might win, fi-om his heing so superior a horse to those he had to run against; and I told Mr. Lake that it was Neale's fault in not treating the horse in a proper manner before he left Newmarket, it being impossible for any man to get Escape well to run in the short time he had then been under Casborne's care. Mr. W. Lake appeared very angry at my declaring that Escape had not been treated properly; and I further observed that Escape's unfitness to run was unpleasant to me, as His Royal Highness had much money depending upon his winning both days. However, as I had come such a great way to ride so good a horse, I would have a little bet upon him, and I took Mr. W. Lake thirty guineas to twenty-five that Escape wins both days.

That 43 was then the betting. I also betted five guineas more the same way with a gentleman who lodged at Mr. Knapton's Coffee-house, and Mr. Knapton kindly paid it for me. I had no other bet whatever on either of those two races in which I rode Escape at York, in 1790. After Escape had been beaten on the second day, Mr. W. Lake told mc that he had edged off all the Prince's money but three hundred and fifty.

Escape was run very hard the first day by a horse that was publicly known to run but very moderately: but the next day Escape was beaten very easily.

A circumstance occurred on the first day of my riding Escape that gave rise to some ill-natured reflections upon my conduct. I rode without spurs; which is very unusual. The reason for it was, that I lis Royal Highness, just before my setting off for York, had given me a pair of spurs; and 1 was (as I ought to be) much pleased with them. I took them, and only them, to York. Just before running I thought the spur were too long long in the neck, and became fearful to ride in them. I knew Escape's free manner of running, and concluded that he would go better without than with those spurs, for that day's race; and it was my intention on the morrow either to ride in tliosq spurs or borrow a pair.

Before I come immediately to the riding of Escape at the October meeting, I must notice the circumstances that happened previous to my riding him, on the 26th of April 1791, at Newmarket, where he ran the Duke's Course (it is something short of four miles) against Skylark, c. and Skylark was backed two to one to win. Escape waited in this race, and won with extraordinary ease.

After His Royal Highness's Baronet had won the Oatlands at Ascot Heath, T. Perron, the train-, ing groom, said Mr. Richard Veinon named it about Newmarket that Chifney had been at his tricks again. This calls lipon me to shew what these tricks were. I likewise wish to make known the very great change Escape made at that time jn his running in five clear clays. This will render it necessary for me to follow Escape closely from his trial till after his race.

On June the 13th, 1791, (being the Monday after Epsom races,) I was at Tattersall's, where Mr. W. Lake communicated to me a letter from Newmarket, stating that the Oatland horses were all well, and asked me what was best to be done with them. I recommended their being ordered up to Epsom immediately, and to run them two miles round Epsom at the same weights as they were to carry for the Oatlands. Mr. W. Lake suggested, that as the horses then were so well to run, would it not be better for them to be tried at Newmarket directly, and then for them to set off for Ascot. I felt it my duty to persist in my first opinion. Mr. Lake continued very much displeased; and then I replied that he might try them at Newmarket if he pleased. I had been asked, and told him what I thought was best to be done, He then turned from me, saying, he cared not where they were tried, or any thing ahout them.

Soon after this, Mr. W. Lake called to me to question me again about the horses, and I remarked, that it was of no use to say what I thought about them, for whatever I did say I was sure to displease him. He then replied, "Whatever you " say is best to be done, shall be done." I repeated my recommendation, and the 21st of June 1791 was fixed to try them at Epsom.

Early on that morning I came from Mickleham, and met Mr. W. Lake at the stable gate upon Epsom Downs, before day-light. I observed that I had made myself lolb. thinking that he would have me ride Escape. " No!" said he in a sharp tone, "I meant you to ride Pegasus; but " I don't care what you ride." I offered immediately to change my weights, observing, that I had made myself the heaviest weight, as I did not know which horse it would be his pleasure I should ride, and had made myself the highest weight,

A7 as I could so much easier reduce than increase my weight at that time of the morning. Mr. Lake seemed much displeased, and said, he cared not what I did. I then made myself ready to ride Pegasus. I was here afraid to recoil against this unfair usage of Mr. Lake's, fearful it might put a stop to the Prince's business.

As soon as it was light enough, the horses ran two miles, at the same weights they were to run at for the Oatlandsj on the Tuesday following, at Ascot Heath. Escape won this trial; he beat Baronet about a neck; Pegasus was beaten a great way, and I think Smoker was beaten more than a hundred yards from Pegasus.

When Escape and Baronet had about three hundred yards to run, they were going by themselves in a very severe manner, and very fast, and Baronet was then running at his utmost, and he could not lay nearer than within about two lengths of Escape; but from Escape's making so very free with himself in most parts of the race, it made him come back to Baronet. I think Escape would would have beaten Baronet three lengths or more if Escape had waited.

These four horses were all in the Oatlands Stakesj at Ascot Heath, on the Tuesday following, at the same weights as they carried in this trial; and to- run the same length of ground (two miles) Escape, 6 years old, carried. Qst. lolbs. Baronet, 6 years old, carried. 8st. 4lbs. Pegasus, 7 years old, carried. Qst. Olbs. Smoker, 4 years old, carried. 7st. Olbs. After this trial I rode part of the way to Sutton with Mr. W. Lake, and asked him to be pleased to bet to the losing of fifty guineas for me that Escape won the Oatlands, at Ascot Heath, on the following Tuesday: begging him not to bet for me on the next day, (being Thursday, and betting-day attattersall's,) but to wait till Monday, as that was betting-day at Tattersall's again: for all the people at Tattersall's would know that the horses had been tried on that day, and that they would be more fearful of betting on the very next day than they would on the following Monday, and that I thought thought it likely to make some hundreds difference in his laying out my fifty guineas.

Mr. Lake asked how they were to know about the horses being tried. I said the horses stood at a public stable, with other horses and boys; the smith was there to plate them, c. it was therefore to be expected that the people would know that the horses had been tried. I told Mr. Lake their knowing it was of little consequence, the chief object being not to let them know what they could do. At this time the bets ran thirty to one against Escape.

On the next day the horses set out for Ascot, and on Sunday afternoon Gaskoin, His Royal Highness's groom at Carlton-House, went with me to see them. Alighting from our horses, Gaskoin went into the house, and I into Escape's loose stable. I found him stripped, and the lad was brushing him over. I instantly saw E! scape was not well to run; and I was very certain that his chance for the Oatlands Stakes was all done away, and entirely so from mismanagement. I then Q went went up to Escape; I coaxed him, kissed him, then left him. I then proceeded to Baronet's loose stable, and I also found him stripped and brushing over. I saw him very well, and I thought he was likely to run for the race as he had done in his trial; and I immediately made up my mind to ride him for the Oatlands; for I thought I would take his chance of winning, after seeing that Escape had none; as I presumed His Royal Highness would allow me to ride which horse I liked, after giving my reasons.

I returned into the house to Gaskoin, where there were several other grooms taking tea, he. Bill Price, His Royal Highness's second training groom, gave me a letter to deliver to Mr. W. Lake, as I was going to London in the morning, and I charged myself with its delivery. When Gaskoin and I were coming away, B. Price desired me to make his duty to Mr. W. Lake, and tell him that Escape was as well to run as a horse could be. I made no answer, and Price repeated it. I was determined not to deliver any such message, message, and therefore endeavoured to appear as if I had not heard it.

I assured Gaskoni how vexed I Vvas at tlie prospect of His Royal Highnesses losing the Oat-land Stakes, upon which more money, I believed, was depending than was ever known upon one race, and this entirely from His Royal High-ness's man that is with the horses not knowing liis business; and what teazed me more so is because I know it, and no other person can be made to know it; so that I am not likely to be believed. But it is not seasonable for me to say any more upon the subject, I wishing to reserve my opinion upon it till 1 had an opportunity of submitting it to His Royal Highness. Gaskoin went to Bag-shot, and I to Egham, where I met with Mr. Sykes the bettor, and took him five hundred to thirty that Baronet won the Oatlands. On my arrival in town the next morning, I instantly wrote a note to Mr. W. Lake, to forbid him to bet any money for me upon Escape, for the Oatlands. I sent it, with Bill Price's letter, by a porter from G 2 Hatchett's

Hatchctt's Hotel, directed to Mr. W. Lake, at Carlton-House.

I then lay down till it was time to go to Tatter-sail's, and there I took Mr. Vauxhall Clark five hundred to twenty-seven that Baronet won the Oatfends. Mr. W. Lake did not come to Tatter-sal Ps that day.

Having returned to Egham to sleep, I was the next morning on the race ground to wait for His Royal Highness, who came on it with Mr. W, Lake, on horseback. I immediately placed myself in sight, and His Koyal Highness called to me, saying, "Sam Chifiiey, come this way. I immediately got up to the side of His Royal Highness and Mr. W. Lake, and His Royal Highness said, "Saui Chifney, I shall run Escape and Baronet only; which do you ride? R ide ' which you please, say which you ride, I am " in a hurry."

I answered His Royal Highness, " that I should " ride Baronet." These were the first words that passed from His Royal Highness to me concerning the horses for the Oatlands. His Royal Highness tlien turned to Mr. W. Lake, and said, "War- wick Lake, Sam Chifney rides Baronet, you " will tell Bill Price to ride Escape." His Royal Highness and Mr. Lake then rode up the course, and soon after, His Royal Highness came riding by liimself, down the course, and asked me what was the meaning of my riding Baronet? " I thought " you intended to ride Escape?" I replied to His Royal Highness, that I had intended riding Escape; but I thought him not well to run, which is my reason for not riding him. His Royal Highness said,- Sam Chifney, Bill Price and " Warwick Lake assure me, that Escape is as well to run as a horse can be." I replied to His Royal Highness, that I believed Bill Price an honest fellow, but he knew no better; and I should be glad if His Royal Highness would not run Escape to-day, for the ground is hard, and I am fearful he should get hurt, for he is a very capital runner; he is clearly a better horse than Baronet at the weights they run to-day; and

Escape 54 Escape is much the host horse in England. Hi3 Royal Highness then left mo, and soon after returned again, and said to mc, that he had seen the groom and Mr. Lake again, and told thenv my thoughts of Escape; they had both repeated, that Escape was as well to run as horse could be; therefore I must run him, Sam Chifney, as I " shall win such a great deal of money if Escape win." I then observed to His Royal Highness, that upon second thoughts I am glad Escape does run, as that would determine it.

His Royal Highness then asked me, if I thought 1 sliould win upon Baronet; I told His Royal Highness that I was fearful; but there being a very great field to run against, I thought that gave me a good chance; I had thought very much of Escape's winning, had he been well. His Royal Highness then told me, he should be glad to see me win upon Baronet, for he should win a great deal of money if he won. I took the liberty of asking His Royal Highness how much His Highness should win as nigh as His Royal Highness

Highness could guess. His Royal Highness said, I think I shall win seventeen thousand." As His Royal Highness was riding from me, I said that I had backed Baronet, and His Royal Highness appeared pleased at my naming it. His Royal Highness rode on, and presently came to see the horses saddled, saw me mounted, wished me good luck, and in "a short time after, Baronet's goodness carried me in first. This was a very hard race with Baronet and Express till within a few yards of the end. My very favourite horse Escape was beaten a great way; for when these horses had near half a mile to run. Baronet at that time was about four lengths behind the front horses. Baronet was there by choice. Escape was at that time about two lengths behind Baronet; but I saw him clearly beaten, and the man was getting very severe upon him. I was about to call to the rider to pull Escape up, but thought better of it, because Escape was not only behind me, but wide from me, and there weie horses between us, and I was fearful of keeping my head turned turned till the rider should hear me, lest my horse's fore legs should get entangled with the other horse's hind legs. I very much wished Escape to be pulled up, that he might not be abused after having been so much beaten. I saw no more of him in this race, but from the situation I left him in, and the front horses renewing their pace, he must have been beaten a very great way. It is to be remarked, thai the same person that trained Escape for the trial and r?. ce rode Escape for trial and race.

Some time after this race was over, Mr. W.

Lake was standing on the course, before the booths, and Gaskoin and I stopped with him.

Mr. Lake said, "Well, Chifney, these horses ran

"the same again." I replied, "Sir!" Mr,

Lake said, "Escape and Baronet, I mean; they ran just the same to-day as they ran in their trial the other day." I said, "The same to- day. Sir, as they ran in their trial the other day?" Mr. Lake added, "Yes, the very same to-day, as they ran in their trial; for Es- cape cape could have been second, ii he had pleased."

The observations which the warmth of my feelings on that occasion forced from me, the collected calmness of my present situation induces ine to suppress. They were uttered in the hearing of Mr. Gaskoin.

This was an astonishing saying of Mr. Lake's, telling me that Escape could have been second if he had pleased. Had he amused himself with telling this falsity to his saddle-horse groom, why perhaps he might not have known that his master had told him a falsity. If Mr. Lake attempts to vindicate himself by saying that Escape's rider saw Baronet could win, that he would not press his horse farther; this could not be; for, a short distance before coming to the winning-post. Express and Baronet's heads were even with each other, and both horses at their utmost,. Express tired first in this severe run, which flung Baronet clear before him just before getting to the winning post, and no one could see that Baronet could H win 58 win till tbis happened. I don't see what this saying could mean of Escape's being second but by Mr. Lake's first trying it upon me, to see if he Gould the better impose it upon the Prince, by way of making it out that he had been right in his standing it out to the Prince, before starting, that Escape was well to run.

It appears to me that Mr. Richard Vernon had been imposed upon in his information by a person that had not an opportunity of knowing of Chif-ney's changing his opinion from riding Escape to ride Baronet, so early as those sort of agents are generally used to, which would disappoint them in their betting, c.; it is ungentlemaning them-, selves to use those dirty little agents that make it their business to hunt after the secrets of noblemen's and gentlemen's stables, such as their private trials, c.

It has been alluded to me that I was tricking Mr. W. Lake, my not telling him my opinion changing from Escape to ride Baronet. I did not like to name it to Mr. W. Lake; for what I 59 had saidto him about horses' condition had made him so very dissatisfied with mc there were many unpleasant appearances to me. I thought Baronet's chance for the Oatlands might be done away by some means, if I made my opinion known. My silence on this I thought was necessary for Baronet's safety, till led out for running.

I had always, till this time, made my opinion known to Mr. Warwick Lake, on the Prince's business, dutifully.

Mr. Richard Vernon" Those are Chifneys tricks again."

Escape stood matched for the 3d of October 1791 against the Duke of Bedford's Grey Dio-med, at even weights, four miles, over New-market, for one thousand guineas. A long time before this match was ran I wished His Royal Highness to bet as much money on Escape, for this race, as His Highness would ever wash to stand on any one race. Before this match came on to be run. Escape was tried across the Flat, which I reckon to be about a mile and a quarter. He H 2 was 60 was tried with Don Quixote and-Lance, and Escape was beaten several lengths by both these horses, before they had run half their course; and Escape was beaten a very great way at the time that Don Quixote and Lance got in, and Lance was bcr. tcn easily by Don Quixote. Li this trial I rode Don Quixote. After the trial was over, as I was going home, Mr. W. Lake asked me if I had any thing to say to His Royal Highness, and if I had been satisfied witli the

horse's running that day, as he was going to write to His Royal Highness at Brighton. I desired my duty to His Royal Highness, and expressed my strongest wishes that he would not bet upon Escape against Grey Diomed, for Escape now could not run in the least; and I wished His Royal Highness would be pleased to give orders for Escape to be tried again before his match. Mr. Lake observed that Escape had run as well this morning as ever, for he never could run any better across the Flata very extraordinary saying of Mr. Lake's, as Escape had been seen at
Epsom
Epsom to run the fastest horse upon the turf, and with Nimble this same course. I replied, that if Escape did not run a great deal better against Grey Diomed than he had run that day, Grey Diomed would run quite away from him. Mr. Lake still persisted in this opinion. I then frankly told Mr. Lake that if he did not choose to inform His Royal Highness what I had said, that I must do it myself, as my duty required.

It appears to me after that His Royal Highness did give orders for Escape to be tried again; for a day or two before the match Mr. W. Lake came from Swaftham races to Newmarket, and he sent Neale, the training-groom to me over-night, de siring me to be ready in the morning to try Escape, provided it should rain in the night. It did not rain, that I knew of, and Escape was not tried.

On the morning of the race (3d of October 1791) Mr. W. Lake came to me when upon the race ground, wishing me to bet with him upon Escape. I told Mr. Lake I certainly should not back Escape; for if he did not run a great deal better better to-day than he did in his trial, Grey Diomecl would run clear away from him. Mr. Lake then left me, and some time after returned, still pressing me to back Escape, which I declined. I now felt myself teazed at being urgently and repeatedly pressed to bet upon Escape, so directly against my desire.

I must here remark, that before I went over to saddle I waited in expectation that His Royal Highness would send for me to question me about Escape, and to receive his orders, c.: but His Royal Highness did not send for me, neither did Mr. W. Lake give me any orders; nor do I to this moment know why His Royal Highness did not see me before starting in this, as he usually did at other races, but this race particularly.

After this, as I was going over the course to get ready to start, and when I was more than half way over the Four-mile Course, Mr. W. Lake rode up to me in a great hurry, and renewed his a. nxiety for me to make a bet upon Escape.

I then observed to Mr. Lake, that I was ashamed ashamed to be the cause of giving him so iiuich trouble concerning my making a bet; therefore, as it was his particular wish, I would bet him twenty guineas tliat Escape won. It was merely to say we were all on one side, either to win a httle or lose a little, whichever might happen. But I begged of him not to let this bet make him imagine that I thought Escape would win; I merely betted to oblige him; and this I desired might be made known to His Royal Highness. Mr. W. Lake turned back, and I went over and got ready to start and run. Escape was just able to win; they were both upon a par a small distance from the end; but Escape being the strong-est horse, it let him just win.

Directly after the race was over, and the horses were walking back to scale, His Royal Highness rode up by the side of Escape, and did me the very high honour of taking me by the hand, saying, "Sam Chifney, no person but you shall ride " for me."

Kind and flattering as these words were from

His Koyal Highness to mc, they notwithstanding created alarm and mistrust in me that attempts had heen made to affect His Royal Highness with impressions unfavourable to me, and tliat it would have been of bad consequence to me if Escaj)e had not won; nor indeed could I ever account for Mr. W. Lake's taking so much pains for me to bet upon Escape.

On the 5th of October 1791 one clear day after this race, Escape and Grey Diomed met to run together again, for a Plate, the same course and at even weights. Some distance before these horses got in, I found that Escape could beat Grey Diomed with great ease; I therefore, by-choice, made a near race of it, and the Judge gave the race to Escape a head only.

When I came from scale, I advised Mr. Lake to match Escape against Grey Diomed, and give him 5lb. or more; telling him that Escape could give Grey Diomed a great deal of weight and beat him I found Escape was coming fast to his capital form, if not overdone in his work to take away his speed; but I heard no more about matching him. But on the evening of the igth of October 1791, I was in Mrs. Brett's bar with Mr. Vaux-hall Clark and several others, when some jierson, I think it was Mr. Bish called over the horses that were entered to run for the plate the next da, amongst which was Escape.

An unpleasant sensation seized me instantly about his being entered, for I was fearful that he should be beaten, being doubtful he was not quite fit to run.

I then went to the coffee-house to see at what time the horses were to start next day; and in going, Mr. V. Clark accompanied me a short distance, and asked if I thought Escape would win to-morrow? I said, "Yes, if he is well!" Mr. Clark replied, in surprise, ' Why is he not " well?" I said, "Yes, he is well, or what they are pleased to call ivell, otherwise the Prince would " not let him be entered; but I mean if he be well to run, he will win; but if he be not well to run, I "he

"he is likely to be beaten, for there is a strong " field to run against."

Mr. Clark appeared to wish to draw me out to speak more explicitly about Escape's not being well, but I said no more about it.

I did not think it little or none improper of Mr. Clark asking me this, as the Prince knowing he sometimes betted for me, and a public horse like this.

I NOW come to the immediate subject of Escape's losing and winning.

On the 20th October 1791? as I was going on the race-ground in company with others, His Royal Highness from on horseback called to me saying, "Sam Chifney, Escape is sure of winning to-day, is not he?" I immediately rode up and informed His Royal tlighness that I did not know that Escape was sure of winning to day.

His Royal Highness said, "Yes, Escape is sure of winning to-day." I then wished His Royal Highness not to back him; for the odds are likely to be high upon him; that His Royal Highness might lose a deal of money to winning very little.

His Royal Highness then turned short from me, saying, "No, I shall not bet upon him, but he is sure of winning;" and immediately joined the company that was riding down the lower side of the running ground to the turn of the lands.

I now found myself under a peculiar embarrassment, for I very much wanted to tell His Royal Highness that I was doubtful about Escape being quite fit to run, and that this was my only reason for wishing His Royal Highness not to bet upon him; jmd yet I thought Escape might win without being quite well to run; therefore, if I made any complaint about Escape's condition, and he should afterwards win, I thought I should be represented by some as mischievous. Those thoughts were what made me so slow in trying to break my opinion to His Royal Highness that I was doubtful about Escape not being fit to run; under these impressions, 1 wished to be well timed in acquainting Elis Royal Highness with my doubts about Escape's fitness to run. Then His Royal Highness turned so very short upon me at the time I was going to make known my opinion; I became fearful that he was tired of hearing me; being conscious that I had been very often troublesome on the like occasions; that 1 immediately became so very much vexed, that the strength of my limbs went from me in so extraordinary a manner, I never felt any thing equal to it before. 1 thought it my duty to offer my ojjinion to the Prince, and I was trained to it from being questioned upon the same.

After there had been a race or two over, His Royal Highness was in the carriage with Lord Barrymore, standing near the lower end of the rails, by the turn of the lands; and I was on horseback, standing at a small, distance from the carriage, when His Royal Highness called to me, and asked me if Escape's race was coming next? I answered, "Yes, your Royal Highness." His Royal Highness said, "Come this Vvay, Sam Chif-" ney, I will give you your orders how to ride " Escape." I immediately got up to the side of the carriage, and His Royal Highness said, "Sam " Chifney, I wish you to make very strong play " with Escape;" then made a pause, as I thought, for me to make answer: I. did not make answer. His Royal Highness then said, "Sam Chifney, I am never afraid when that I am giving South

"and you orders, for I know you are both too " good jockeys to over-mark your horse; but now 1 will not compel you to make play with " Escape; providing there should be good play made by any other horse, you may wait with " Escape; but should there be no other horse " make such as you think good play, you must " take care to make good play with Escape. I " hope, Sam Chifney, you perfectly understand. I said, "Yes, your Royal Highness, I perfectly " understand." His Royal Highness then ordered the carriage to drive to the betting-post.

Mr. W. Lake had been standing with his horse in his hand, near to the carriage, but on the other side of the rails, whilst His Royal Highness was giving me my orders how to ride Escape.

Directly the carriage was gone, I was then passing near to Mr. W. Lake: he said, "Well, "Chifney, has the Prince given you orders how f to ride Escape?" I said, "Yes, Sir." Mr. W. Lake said, "What are your orders?" I told

Mr. Lake that His Royal Highness wished me to make very strong play with Escape; but after, His Royal Highness gave me leave to wait with Escape, providing there should be any other horse make good play; but should there be no other horse make such as I thought good play, that I must take care to make good play with Escape.

Mr. W. Lake then asked me if I thought that the best way for Escape to run? I replied, "No, "Sir; if I had my life depending upon Escape's " winning to-day, I should wish Escape to wait " by all means; but as His Royal Highness told me he should not bet upon him, and as I am " so often contradicting my orders, and as I was not asked my opinion, I thought it would " be impertinent of me to offer to give His Royal " Highness any more trouble."

Mr. Lake said, ' Well, Chifney, I think as you " do, that Escape had better wait, so you will wait at all events; and I see the Prince's car-

Explained in page 78.

riage

"liage, I will go immediately and make every " thing perfectly pleasant."

I immediately went over to sadile; when I was saddling Escape, I asked if he liad had a sweat since he ran last; and I was answered that he had not had a sweat since his last running against Grey Diomed. The horses started, I waited with Escape, and was beaten.

Immediately that the race was over. Escape pulled up to walk back to scale. His Royal Highness came up to me, saying, "Sam Chifney, you " have lost this race by not making strong play " with Escape, as I desired you." I answered, I don't know that I have, your Royal High-" ness." His Royal Highness then said, "Yes, you certainly have lost the race by not making " strong play with Escape " I then hoped His Royal Highness had not lost much money upon the race. His Royal Highness said, "No, I " have not lost a stiver: but that don't argue, " for Escape certainly would have won, if you " had made strong play with him, as I desired 73 ' you; and I do tell you, Sam Chifney, that I " am a better jockey than Mr. Lake and you " both, for you have lost the race by not running " as I desired you." His Royal Highness turned from me, for I was got to the scale-house to light and weigh.

Whilst I was in the weighing-house, I received a message to attend His Royal Highness. Immediately I got my clothes on I went immediately to His Royal Highness, who was on horseback with Mr. W. Lake, standing close to the farther winning-post of the Beacon Course. His Royal Highness said, ' Sam Chifney, what is the mean-" ing of Escape's being beaten to-day, for you " tell me that Escape is the best horse in the " world?" I replied, ' I did tell your Royal " Highness that Escape was much the best horse " in England, and I think the same of him now, your Royal Highness." His Royal Highness continued, "Sam Chifney, tell me your motive immediately why Escape is beaten to-day." K ' I will 74 I will tell)our Royal Highness my motive immediately why I think Escape is beat to day. It is a fortnight, or a fortnight and a day, I tiiink, since Escape ran last, which was with " Grey Dicmed. During that time Escape has not had a sweat, neither has he been tried " since, but he has been tenderly treated; and ' notwithstanding he looks straight and hand-" some to the eye, he is unfit to run; and this " I believe is the reason of his being beat to- day your Royal Elighness." His Royal Highness said, "Very well." I then bowed, and drew back to a small distance, facing his Royal Highness and Mr. Lake, not knowing whether His Royal Highness had quite done with me; and while I was thus waiting, I heard His Royal Highness or Mr. Lake say something about Escape's running to-morrow. I immediately took the liberty of asking His Royal Highness if Escape were to run to-morrow. His Royal Highness said, "Yes, I certainly shall run Escape to-morrow."

I said.

75 I said, "I am vciy glad your Royal Highness does run Escape to-morrow, for I think Es-" cape will win to-morrow; and I wish your " Royal Highness to back liim

to-morrow to " losing six or seven hundred; and I wish you to ' back him, Mr. Lake, and I will back him, your " Royal Highness: and had Escape not run to-" day, I should not have wished your Royal High-" ness to back him to-morrow, for this sharp rally " to-day will not fatigue him; it has caused a " good perspiration, so as to lighten him of his " flesh, and opened his pores, that he will run both faster and longer to-morrow; and his " running to-day is my only reason for wishing your Royal Highness to back him to-morrow; " for had he not run to-day, I should not have " wished your Royal Highness to back him to-" morrow."

This is all that passed upon the subject this day.

I wish it to be understood that I don't mean that horses are always to run better the second day

K 2 than than the first; it is condiitionally. My motive for wishing His Royal Highness to bet to losing six or seven hundred was, 1 thought that sum as much as I could wish His Royal. Highness to risk upon my thoughts about Escape being likely to run. better the second day, from Escape's running the first day. I heard His Royal Highness the Prince of Wales name twice, to gentlemen at Newmarket, on the day after Escape's second running, viz. the 2Jst of October 1791, the exact sum His Royal Highness the Prince of Wales betted upon Escape on the 21st of October 1791-It was under four hundred guineas, and it was near four hundred guineas.

Upon full reflection on past circumstances, I conceive that it may be necessary to throw in an explanatory thought or two upon my changing my orders, after I had received orders from His Royal Highness in person; and this more especially, as I had some time before intimated to His Royal Highness that I was afraid of riding to Mr. W.

Lake's 77 Lake's orders; and that I wished it could be made His Royal Highness's pleasure that I should receive orders from any other person than Mr. Lake.

Vvhen at the carriage, His Royal Highness said he wished for Escape to make very strong play, and made a pause, as I thought, for me to make an answer; but from what had occurred at first coming upon the course, likewise His Royal Highness's speaking in so firm a manner when I was at the carriage, that notwithstanding I so very much wanted to tell His Royal Highness my thoughts; but as they were something like a contradiction, I was fearful to name them, without it was His Royal Highness's pleasure to ask for them, as I particularly wished for Escape to wait, and for His Royal Highness to have known my reasons, (and none else,) to prevent any bad constructions being hawked about, of what I wanted to say about Escape's condition, provided Escape won, I must observe, that when I last parted from His Royal Highness I did not go to Mr. W. Lake, thinking to change my orders that I received from His Royal Highness. I stopped with Mr. W. Lake, thinking it ill-mannerly to pass him without stopping, as he apparently waited for me to stop. Then Mr. W. Lake questioning me, and his thinking as I did, that Escape had better wait, saying that he would go immediately to His Royal Highness, and make every thing perfectly pleasant; and as I thought it so very necessary for Escape to wait, I thought I would agree to it, believing that His Royal Highness would think that I had some particular reasons, and that His Royal Highness would be sufficiently satisfied till the race was over to know my motives; and let the race come off which ever way it happened, I thought for certain that His Royal

Highness would be perfectly satisfied with my conduct. As to what I have before said about contradicting orders, (in Page 71J I meant merely merely to infer, tliat as I did not always think as His Royal Highness and Mr. W. Lake did, with their first naming my orders, I had sometimes expressed a contrary wish, from which I might be thought refractory or contradictory: but I meant not to hint at my riding Scota at Lewes, or Pegasus at Newmarket, against Mr. W. Lake's orders, for these facts I never made known to His Royal Highness.

It is much rumoured that Chifncy will be master, and, in other words that he will ride as he hkes, and that he is obstinate and opinionated. I don't like to be thought thus undutiful. I lived with Thomas Panton, Esq. four years, and left his service to come into the Prince's service. At the time of my living with Mr. Panton I rode most of the Duke of Bedford's horses from J 787 to 1790, and Mr. Panton told me that the Duke of Bedford was the very best pleased with my riding his horses, as I always rode to a T, as his Grace told me.

I seldom I seldom had strict orders to ride but from the Duke of Bedford, and His Grace had a particular pleasure in having his horses run strict to his orders; and where I had but slight orders in my riding I was the more open to faults in the opinion of others. My being accused of obstinacy,-c. must proceed from my keeping to my own opinion when once taken, and not explaining all my thoughts on the subject: and, in my profession and situation, it was not always proper for me to say every thing I thought, for it would both offend and teach others in my profession.

In running the race on the 20th of October I waited with Escape, and Coriander won. Some yards before Coriander got to the winning-post, I gave over running with Escape, and at that time Skylark, I think, was beaten about two lengths by Coriander; Escape at that very time was beaten by Skylark three parts of his neck; and Pipeator, I think, was a length or two behind Escape. I do not vouch for the exact order in which these horses horses came in. As Escape had been very much beaten, I gave over, a few 3ards before he got in, from forcing him, and paid no attention to which of the beating horses passed the post first of Escape and Pipeator.

This race was from the Ditch-in, which is called two miles, and there was but little running made till they got a small distance over the turn of the lands; they then made a sudden start into very severe running, and continued so all the way in.

From where they set into this very severe run ning was, I think, rather more than half a mile from the winning-post. Soon after they started into this very severe running, Escape in a veiy little time was some little farther behind than I wished him to be, and it frightened me at the time, thinking I had been too tender with him; but I soon saw it was not so, but that Escape could not run as fast as Coriander or Skylark. Escape was at no time in this race able to get up L to -to Skylark's head; I mean from the time they set into severe running. At no one time of my riding do I remember any horse to have so many severe runs as Escape had in this race, trying to beat Skjlark. Coriander was running first, and to the left of Skylark; Escape was running to the right of Skylark; and I am confident that had I been riding any other horse than Escape in this race, I should have given over running sooner than I did, if I had felt that other horse as much beaten as Escape was. The different changes which I perceived in Escape's running I at the time believed to be from improper management. I was not so uneasy at his losing, as His Royal Highness did not suffer by it; and I thought that Escape would run as well as ever when he was fit to run.

When His Royal Highness told me that he was a better jockey than Mr. W. Lake and me both, those words I thought were meant as forgiveness for my riding contrary to orders, and I bowed and laughed; I meant as thanks; particularly so, because because His Royal Highness thought I had lost the race by it.

On the 21st of October 1791, when I was on the race-ground, His Royal Higlmess came to me near or in the Round Course,, over against the Well Gap, as there had been a race over some part of the Round Course before Escape's coming on. His Royal Highness then said, "Sam Chif-" ney, I will give you your orders again to-day; " and let me beg of you to take care that you make no mistake to-day. I wishj Sam Chif-" ney, for you to make play with Escape to-day; " but I will not compel you to make play to-day. " Should there be tolerable good play made by " any other horse, you may then wait with Es-" cape; but should no other horse make tolerable good play, you must make tolerable good play " with Escape. God bless yon 1" As His Royal Highness was leaving me, I said, "I wish your " Royal Highness to back Escape;" and he called tome, saying, "Yes, I will."

1-2 I then I then went to the Round Course Stand-house, and waited till Mr. W. Lake came down; when I told him that His Royal Highness had given me orders how to ride Escape, and told him I would thank him to lose twenty guineas for me upon Escape. Mr. Lake said, "No, I will have no- thing to do with it, there are so many unplea-" sant things happen."

Some yards from this I waited for F. Small-man's coming up to me to give me another hack. Smallman then lived with mehe is a relation of mine. I told Smallman that Mr. Lake had refused betting twenty guineas for me upon Escape, and that I durst not go over to ride till I had given some person orders to bet for me, for I had pledged myself to His Royal Highness to back Escape; " and His Royal Highness, after the race is over, is very likely to give me joy of my winnings, or say he is sorry for my losing, whichever happens, and asking how much I won or lost; then for me to say I had no bet, 85 why His Royal Highness will not know what those things can mean, where that I first be- fore a race advise His Highness to bet, and say I shall back the horse, then the horse gets " beat, and I tell His Royal Highness I had no bet " upon him." I complained to Smallman that when I told one to bet for me, he generally made it known to the betting-ring that he was betting for me, which might change the betting so as to make His Royal Highness have some hundreds the worst of his bets, and all from my having betted twenty guineas.

But I durst not go over without ordering some person to bet for me; " and as chief of my bets this summer has been with Mr. Vauxhall Clark, I will not change him for this once." I thought the field knew that Mr, Clark sometimes betted for me; that seeing him bet on Escape, the odds were likely to change the sooner; so I desired him to go to Mr. Clark, and tell him to lose twenty guineas for me upon Escape; and assure him that 86 His Royal Highness intended to back his horse, and that I begged of him not to make the least offer of a bet about Escape till he was certain that His Royal Highness had done betting; for if he did, and I knew it, I would never bet with him more. I directly went over to saddle and start. Skylark chose to make play, and I waited with Escape, and Escape won.

As I came from scale, I was told Mr. W. Lake had been saying something severe to His Royal Highness concerning Escape's winning. I made it therefore my business to go immediately to His Royal Highness, who was riding with a gentleman near the Great Stand-house, when His Royal Highness accosted me in the following words: " Sam Chifney, as soon as Escape's race was over, Mr. Lake came up to me, and said, I " give your Royal Highness joy, but I am sorry " the horse has won; I would sooner have given " a hundred guineas. I told Mr. Lake that I " did not understand him j that he must explain

"himse r."

87 himself." I tlien made His Royal Highness answer, saying, "Yes, your Royal Highness, it is very necessary he should explain himself." This was all that passed on the subject to-day. I have been informed that His Royal Highness called to a gentleman, when in the betting-ring, in the hearing of all the bettors, saying, that he had better not bet against Escape, for "Sam Chifney says Escape will run better to-day than he did yesterday."

Whilst I was saddling Escape to-day, I believed Jie had not been set upon muzzle, or that he had been improperly filled, and I feared His Royal Highness would lose all the money he betted upon hinis and my opinion sacrificed. The betting, indeed, greatly confirmed my surmise. The betting was four and five to one against Escape; and on all such occasions the field judges by one or two men's manner of betting, that there is something wrong that runs the odds up so high.

In addition to the remarks I have already made, I cannot 1 cannot entertain a doubt but tliat from His Royal Highness's backing Escape,; c. Escape would have been the first favourite, had he been brought out to run as he ought to have been. This race was four miles, and Skylark made strong play, anjl was first, as near as I can guess, till the last hundred yards, or less, of the winning-post. Skylark there stopped short, and gave over running from distress. Escape and another horse passed him; and, from Skylark stopping so very short, the horses that had to persevere in were likely to beat Skylark in several lengths. From what I felt of Escape in this race, before he passed Skylark, I don't know that Escape could have beat Skylark in this race had they both run this race upon an equal advantage; but a much better horse, if well, than Skylark.

Skylark was fast, a slug, and a jade, which was very much against him, his making strong play over the Four-mile Course.

Mr. W. Lake's conduct concerning Escape's second second day's running was confessing to His Royal Highness that he had chose to put bad constructions upon what he had heard me say to His Royal Highness on the day before, why I thought Escape was beat on that day, and why I thought Escape would win on the following day.

Some years after this, Casborne was dismissed at Newmarket for supposing him poisoning horses for their races; being concerned with those breaking into noblemen's stables, the night before running, to give the horse, as was supposed, opium balls; and it is believed Casborne had done it for many years.

Mr. W. Lake, Neale, and Casborne had the management of His Royal Highness's horses till His Royal Highness left the turf in 1791.

In 1797? it vvas reported among the noblemen and gentlemen of the turf, that poison balls had been given by Casborne to Escape before he ran with Coriander, Skylark, and Pipeator, on the 20th of October 1791.

But I had no thoughts of Escape's being poisoned; my thoughts why Escape was beat are seen in page 74; and from his being such a very good runner, and his Jiesh and pores being lightened and cleansed on the day before: and under the disadvantageous manner in which Skylark ran this race, Escape might (as he did on this second day) beat Skylark with his belly full; although I readily admit that Escape's winning with his belly full must have greatly surprised those who knew that he had been improperly filled for the race. Then, from Mr. W. Lake's and Neale's infernal conduct, directly the race was over, to the Prince and me, the public might very well believe I had lost upon Escape on the day before intentionally; for directly Escape's race was over, Mr. W. Lake, in the presence of the company, was impudent to the Prince of Wales because Escape had won; and I am told Nealc rode amongst the noblemen and gentlemen, saying, that he hoped their eyes were open now; that it was plain enough now that that he was robbed of forty guineas that he had betted yesterday upon Eseae.

Now the appearance to ine is this: On the first day of Escape's running, Ncale had not sufficient skill to know Escape was not in proper condition to enable him to run near his best form, and he backed him, cried, and was rude.

Whether that severe saying of Mr. W. Lake to His Royal Highness the Prince of Wales directly Escape had won, on the 21st of October 1791, was meant thinking it would cause His Royal Highness to be under the necessity of dismissing Chifney, I will leave Mr. W. Lake to determine.

M 2 Occurrencrs

Occujrences on the Day Jul hiving my riding Escape, on the 2st October 1791.

On the 22cl October 179, in the morning-after Escape had won. His Royal Highness sent for me into his dressing room, and then ordered me to be shown into an adjoining room, where he thus accosted me:" Sam Chifney, I have sent for you upon very unpleasant business. I " am told, Sam Chifney, that you won six or " seven hundred pounds upon the race on the " day before yesterday, where you rode Escape, ' and was beat upon him."

I replied, that I believed His Koyal Highness had not such an opinion of me.

His Royal Highness continued: " I am told,

Sam Cliifney, that you won six or seven Imu- dred pounds upon the race yesterday, where you rode Escae, and won upon him: I am told that Vauxhall Clark won all the money for you." I answered, "May I not offend by " asking who it was that dared to tell your Royal " Highness so?" His Royal Highness replied,. " Sam Chiftiey, I wish to know if you liave any " objection to take your affidavit, naming all the bets you had upon the race, every way, when " you rode Escape, and was beaten upon him, on the day before yesterday?" I acknowledged my readiness to do it, if it would give His Roya Highness any satisfaction. His Royal Highness said, "Sam Chifney, your doing it will give yourself satisfaction, it will give the public sa- tisfaction, and it will give me satisfaction. " You will specify, in your affidavit, all the bets " you had upon both days' races, when that you " rode Escape on the day before yesterday, and " was beat upon him; and yesterday, when that you rode Escapcj and won upon him; naming all the bets you had upon both those races, and " to take your affidavit as such. I hope, Sam " Chifney, you do not misunderstand me." I answered, that I did perfectly understand, and would take care to do as His Royal Highness had ordered me.

His Royal Highness said, Sam Chifney, I " wish to know if you have any objection to be examined by the Jockey Club, and in any way that they are pleased to think proper." I told His Royal Highness that I was very willing to be examined in any way that His Royal Highness or the Jockey Club were pleased to think proper. His Royal Highness then said, "I am told, Sam-" Chifney, that you were arrested, at Ascot " Heath, for 300l., and that Vauxhall Clark paid the money for you." I replied, that this was the first word I had ever heard upon the subject. His Royal Highness said, "Sam Chif-" ney, I wish to know if you have any objection to taking your affidavit that you were not ar- rested at Ascot Heath, neither did Vauxhall Clark pay 300l. for you?" I replied to His Royal Highness, "I am very willing to do it. His Royal Highness said, "Then you will do it. " Good morning!" and then left me.

The malicious invention of the false tale about my being arrested, and Mr. Clark's paying money for me, I believe must be to saddle me with obligation; and, from my being under obligation, it might be their thoughts it would compel me to improper connexion.

When I say the chief of my bets, this summer, had been with Vauxhall Clark, those bets were at other races, not at Newmarket; and why I betted more with Mr. Vauxhall Clark than with any other person, upon His Royal Highness's horses, was, that Mr. Clark chose to take more pains to put himself in my way at times as I thought were seasonable for me to bet without disturbing or offending His Royal Highness's and Mr. Lake's betting, which was generally about sacklling-time, as then I thought His Royal Highness and Mr. W. Lake were likely to have tinished, or nearly finished.

At Newmarket, the horses generally go out to startj and run back. I generally betted there with Mr. W. Lake upon His Royal Highness's horses, as the great betting there is most at the time of the rider's going over the course to saddle, start, and run; and I wished to avoid troubling Mr. W. Lake with my bets as much as I thought was proper, considering Mr. W. Lake had His Royal Highness's bets and his own to ma-nnge. I often went without bets for this reason. I never received the value of one farthing from Mr. Vauxhall Clark, not against any horse that I ever trained or rode, where the above-men-mentioned horse was beat, nor in no other way, of Mr. Vauxhall Clark, that is the least improper.

On the same morning (22d of October 1790 His Royal Highness called to me across the bet- 07 ling-ring. I instantly obeyed his commands, and His Royal Highness put me between himself and Sir Charles Bunbilry, and then rode out upon the Heath. After His Royal Highness and Sir Charles had talked upon the subject His Royal Highness said, "Sam Chifney, I think you told me that you were willing to be examined by the Stewards of the Jockey Club in any way they " please to think proper?"

1 said, "Your Highness, I am proud to meet " any man upon the subject." His Royal Highness then addressed himself to Sir Charles Bun-bury: " There, Sir Charles, you hear him say that he is proud to meet any man upon the " subject. Now, Sir Charles, I

beg of you to " take every pains you possibly can, so as to make " yourselves perfectly satisfied; then inclose me Sam Chifney's affidavits, and apprise me hov, " the business ends, as I am going to Brighton " to-night." His Royal Highness left Sir Charles, and rode near the betting-ring, where N after 9S after he stood a little while, he said, "Sam " Chifncy, this business should be explained." I answered, Your Royal Highness, I don't know how to explain it." His Royal Highness then rode off the turf to town, before the day's 'sport was finished, and I immediately went home. Soon after this I reeeived from Mr. Weatherby, Clerk to the Jockey Club, copies of affidavits, which I swore before the Reverend Dr. Frampton, naming that I had no bet upon the race when I rode Escape on the 20th of October J 791, and that I! iad twenty guineas, and no more, betted upon Escape on the following day, when I rode him on the 21st of October 1791 J and that I had the same desire of winning upon Escape, when I rode him on the 20th of October 1791, as I had when I rode him the following ilay, the 21st of October 1791; and further, that I never had been arrested at Ascot Heath; and that Mr. Vauxhall Clark never did pay any jnoney for me. When I had sworn these affidavits.

99 vlts, they were signed by the Reverend Dr. Frampton, and I immediately returned theip back to Mr. Weatherby.

I was then had up before the Stewards of the Jockey Club, who were

Sir Charles Bunbury, Bart.

Ralph Button, Esq.

Thomas Panton, Esq. Sir Charles asked me some few questions; what bets I had upon the first day's race, when I rode Escape on the 20th of October 1791; and what bets I had upon the race, when 1 rode Escape oil the following day, when he won; and who made my bets for me. I answered, that I had no bet upon the first day's race; that I betted twenty guineas upon Escape the next day, and no more; and that Vauxhall Clark betted for me.

Sir Charles Bunbury then asked me what was my motive for waiting with Escape on the first day. I told Sir Charles Bunbury that he was a wrong judge of his man.

Sir Charles Banbury now stopped, looking about apparently dissatisfied.

Mr. Button said, ' I think Chifney spoke very " fair." Mr, Panton immediately said, "Yes, very fair."

Sir Charles Bunbury did not ask me any more questions.

I then said to Sir Charles Bunbury and the two other gentlemen, that my motive for waiting with Escape was because I knew he could run very fast, I likewise knew that Skylark could run fast, though a jade, for I liad rode against him most of the races he had run.

I was now dismissed; and this is every thing that passed vith me, from and to the Prince of Wales, Mr. W. Lake, and the Jockey Club, on this subject, at Newmarket.

Sir Charles Bunbury might think me too dry or too harsh in my answer to him; but it is to be vecollccted that at this time I had made an affidavit, and answered every particular. That must have have satisfied every candid man. This question of Sir Charle's, to know my motives for waiting with Escape, went into private trials and abilities. The other two stewards well knew this, and they at this time could see that Sir Charles had been wrong in his severely censuring me for being beat on Escape r because, after the Prince had left the race-ground on the 22d of October 1791? and as I was riding home, a nobleman came up to me, and I almost immediately asked him if he could tell me what it was that they were about, or who it was that was making all this disturbance; and this noblemun said it was Sir Charles Bunbury's doing; that it was him that had said so much about it, that caused this disturbance about Escape. When this nobleman came up to me, I knew nothing more than what had fallen from the Prince. These were my reasons for my telling Sir Charles that he was a wrong judge of his man. The other two stewards of course spoke from these same reasons, when they told

Sir Charles that they thought Chifney spoke very fair.

My motive for waiting with Escape may be collected from the foregoing statement (in page 48); as for instance, where Escape carried such extra ordinary high weights, giving Baronet 20lb. and beating him; and yet Baronet, after having been beaten on this trial by Escape, won every thing he ran for that summer; for, on the Tuesday after that trial, (28th June lQl,) Baronet won the Otlands stakes at Ascot Heath, forty-one nominations, one hundred guineas each, against eighteen of the best picked horses that drew up for starting. On the IQth of July he won the King's plate, at Winchester. On the 4th of August he did the same at Lewes; and on the 24th of August he did the like at Canterbury.

And on the 6th of October 1791, Baronet won the King's plate at Newmarket, beating Coriander at even weights. On the 20th, therefore, of this same month (October 1790 I particularly wished

Escape

Escape to wait against Coriander Skylark, Pipe-ator, for two reasons; my first reason was, that I had seen Escape run clear faster than Baronet, p-iving him 20lb. Now Escape in this race only gave Coriander 4lb.; therefore, as Baronet could beat Coriander at even weight, it was natural to expect that Escape should run faster than Coriander; and therefore Escape ought to have waited. My second reason was, my doubting Escape was not quite fit to run; this rendered his waiting particularly necessary, as his condition might make him less able to bear hardship in strong running; and his trial with Baronet, c. before Ascot-Heath races, proved to me that Escape was the fastest runner in England; there can be no other reason wanting why I thought it was D-iost proper that Escape should wait.

I could have told Sir Charles Bunbury this, but I thought it improper then to enter iato such details.

I have I have before remarked, in page 68, that when His Royal Highness gave me orders to make very strong play with Escape; my thoughts pressed so fast upon my mind, that I could not express myself to my own satisfaction. I then wished to have said to His Royal Highness, that I should like for Escape to wait were he quite fit to itin; but as I was doubtful about his being quite fit to run, it became the more necessary for him to wait. I seldom troubled His Royal Highness about the horses, trials, weights, c. as he never appeared to me anxious to be informed of these particulars, leaving such matters to the judgment and direction of Mr. W. Lake.

I had always waited with Escape in all his races I rode him; neither do I remember ever having received orders how to ride Escape, but once before these orders that His

Royal Highness gave me in person, as I have before related but when Escape ran with Skylark in the Spring

Mr. W. Lake then gave ine orders to make play with Escape; but as Skylark chose to make good play, I waited with Escape.

As to Escape's variations in running, Mr. W. Lake well knew every thing that fell from me why I thought Escape made those sudden changes in his running; he knew the very great change Escape had made in his running in five clear days in the month of June, between his trial at Epsom and his running for the great stakes at Ascot, c. And if on the 20th and 21st of October 1791 there were any change in Escape's running for the better, it was not any ways equal to the change Escape had made for the better in his two days' running, a fortnight before this, against Grey Diomed; and Mr. W. Lake knew this directly I came from scale, for I then told him to match Escape against Grey Diomed.

I have again referred to these facts, with a view to deprive Mr. W. Lake and Neale of any justification or even palliation of this conduct on the o course.

io6 course, when they so unwarrantably endeavoured to impress the pabhc with the idea that I intentionally lost the race on the 20th of October 1791 against Coriander, Skylark, and Pipeator. Seen in page 90.

In no place that I have had the honor of living since J 784, have I won a guinea against any horse that was beat where that I either trained or rode him.

In August 184 I had the honor of living with Lord Grosvenor, and I rode his Lordship's horse Fortitude, at York, against Faith and Recovery, c. c. I backed Faith against Recovery, one win or no bet, and Faith won. I saw, before starting, that Fortitude's condition would not allow him to run, I did not conceive that I was acting improperly in making this bet of a few guineas. Lord Grosvenor was not there, and I believe never knew it. Had Lord Grosvenor been there, I don't know I should have mentioned it to his Lordship about Fortitude being unfit 107 to run, for I had found my mentioning these things made the training-grooms and others speak very disrespectfully of me; and I likewise saw they were to be believed before me, which tired me to mention any thing about a horse's condition, but at times when I believed it to be very necessary.

Some argue that Chifney's business is riding, and that he can have no business to say any thing about the training-groom in his horses' condition. Now if my master ask me any questions about his horses, or that I see a likelihood of my master losing his money, either from the training-groom being a dolt or a rascal in his bringing the horse to the post to run, am I to be that undutiful wretch not to tell my master? and if I do, I must offend a dolt and a rascal, and his colleagues of sharpers and be abused by them, and saddled with falsehoods. But I am not that tardy, worthless, cowardly knave to be thus withheld from my master.

08 Then it is tried another waythey argue thus! how is Chifney to know about the horses so well as Neale, as Neale feeds and works the horses, and that Chifney sees the horses but now and then as they are on the exercise-ground? This arguing is likely to serve those that must know less about the management of a horse for running than Neale does. Noblemen and gentlemen cannot know about a horse being thoroughly fit for running, it can only be known from practice with genius. I was brought up under

the best training groom then on the turf, Fox, and Mr. Foley's groom, Mr. Richard Prince. I went to live with Iiim in 1771, (it was the second year of my being in the race-horse stables,) and in 1773 I could ride horses in a better manner in a race, to beat others, than any person ever knew in my time. In 175 I could'train horses for running better than any person I ever yet saw. Riding I learned myself, and training I learned from Mr. Richard Prince; and where horses are trained by dolts that lliat have been brought up under coblers, there is much room for me to know more of the horses being fit or unfit for running, that they train, than they do themselves, if nothing unfair. I don't talk to grooms about horses; what I Iiave to say about liorses, I say to the noblemeii and gentlemen. This has occasioned me to be very much hated and abused by those of this profession and their colleagues; noblemen and gentlemen, however, might soon stop those abuses. When their servants are represented to them that their conduct is scandalous, they should make a strict enquiry into their conduct, and if the servant is in fault, he should be discharged; if not, the rascally author should be given up, and means used to make him suffer Dutiful servants might then live with comfort.

The report of Escape's having been poisoned for the race on the 20th of October 1791 brings to my mind what Mr. Hodges, the great bettor, told me since this race of Escape's, viz. that if I continued continued betting as I did, it would be impossible for me to have a guinea left; saying, that I always backed my judgement in horses;, but that I ought to back men, not horses, for I should have no chance if I continued backing horses. Mr. Hodges's observations were no check to me in betting, though I found his words afterwards come true; yet had Mr. Hodges been able to speak more plainly to me, I should not have backed men. It shewed itself afterwards that Mr. Hodges saw there was much danger to be feared from some means, and it turned out that there was a gang attendant on the turf who make it their business to learn which horse is likely to be the favourite at the betting, and then, by having or procuring access to the stables, the night before running, they give those favourite horses)oison balls, to prevent them running on the following day near their proper form. If these balls have produced their desired eftect, after the race is over those privy to this diabolical practice have an artful artful way (apparently to me since) of duping most of the public by hawking it about that the reason the horse was beaten was, that the day, or the ground, or the length he had run, c. c. did not suit him; and often saddle innocent people with some bad management. When it has been my lot to ride such races where those balls had been given, or any other bad or unskilful management, they generally saddled me with riding a cheat. It has clearly appeared to me that this Casborne and his gang had a person or two that could come to Newmarket, c. and strip all, according as people betted with them and their agents. But all this, I believe, is put a stop to, where that grooms are not indolent, or rascals. I believe I have suffered more than any one by this thieving-trap.

After my examination at Newmarket by the Stewards of the Jockey Club, and I well know that it was after the Duke of York's coming from abroadro7? j the Puchess, that this subject was renewed.

renewed. As I received a letter at Newmarket from Sir John Lade for me to attend on the Prince immediately, at Carlton-House, I went directly to Carlton-House, and the Prince of Wales told me that Sir Charles Bunbury came to him and told him, that if he suffered Chifney to ride his horses, that no gentleman would start against him. His Royal Highness said, he told Sir Charles Bun-bury that if he, or any person, could make it appear that Sam Chifney had done wrong, that he would never speak to him again; and without that, he would not sacrifice him for any person. His Royal Highness then said he should leave the turf, as he could not be guilty of that ingratitude to let his horses start for their engagements, to go over for their forfeits, after being told that no gentleman will start against him, but that he should pay their forfeits, and leave the turf His Royal Highness then said he could seethe meaning of it. " They think you, Sam Chifney, a good rider, " and they think you have won a race or two for

"me that you had no business to have won, and " that there are others who wish to have you, " and others who think you too good for me, as ' they know you will, not see me robbed." His Royal Highness then told me, he should be always glad to see me, and for my own sake to let him see me often; and if he ever kept horses again, that I should train and manage them. After this I was ordered to attend His Royal Highness at Sir John Lade's, in Piccadilly, which I did, and, in the presence of Sir John Lade and Mr. F. C. Phylips, His Royal Highness put his hand upon his bosom and said, that he believed Sam Chifney had been to him very honest, and wished me to understand that the two hundred guineas a year he gave me was for his life; saying, "I cannot ' give it for your life, Sam Chifney, I can only " give it for my own life." I answered His Royal Highness, that I was the same satisfied.

N. B. Till this I thought the salary had been for my own life.

I AM now going to refer to some recent facts, which furnish the most positive proofs that the malicious misrepresentations of my conduct in riding Escape, on the 20th and 21st of October sjgi, still operate most cruelly upon me; so that the publication of this narrative is indispensably necessary.

I trained and rode for Lord Sackville from 794 to 1798, and his Lordship told me, on the morning after his horse Kit Carr had been running, that he was told at the Jockey-Club diimer, by Mr. Wilson and Mr. Upton, (I mean Mr. Christopher Wilson,) that I did not try to win upon him. This was the last time of Kitt Carr's running: it was the Round Course; and before starting; I told Lord Sackville that Kitt Carr was the best runner of the race he was going to run in; but I thought Kitt Carr not quite well in condition condition to run, which might beat him, and I wished his Lordship to bad; the field against Bennington, (as his Lordship had told me that Bennington was the first favourite,) as I thouglit if Kitt Carr failed, that the Uuke of Grafton's Minion was likely to beat Bennington, and that I should like to bet twenty guineas with his Lordship the same way. I thought his Lordship left me with these intentions.

When the race was over, it turned out that Lord Sackville had backed Kitt Carr (only), and for a smart sum which made Kitt Carr come the first favourite.

Gas won, the Duke of Grafton was second, and Kitt Carr was beat several lengths from the first two; but Kitt Carr was able to beat Bennington two or three lengths.

Bennington was Mr. Wilson's horse. Most likely he and his friend Mr. Upton spoke from his rider or groom, who were two extraordinary characters 5 his groom was Casborne, and his rider Casborne's colleague.

I did my utmost to win this abovementioned race upon Kitt Carr, and had the same desire of winning this said race with Kitt Carr as I ever had to win any race that I had ever rode.

I thought his Lordship would mean for me to stand my twenty guineas the same as his Lordship betted and I offered to pay his Lordship twenty guineas, but he did not choose to take it.

In the year 1799 the Earl of Oxford assured me that he had been informed that I rode his horse Polyanthus booty, over Newmarket, for the Oatlandsin 1795.

I did my utmost to win the above race with Polyanthus; and I had the same desire of winning this last-mentioned race with Polyanthus as I ever had to win any race I ever rode.

So little is the truth of the affiiir known of Escape's running, on the 20th of October i79U at Newmarket, that at Brighton races 1800, there was a young member of the Jockey Club, who saw me ride there, and, with other members of 117 the Club, said he was astonished at seeing that rogue Chifney suffered to ride, as he rode Escape at Newmarket. I was informed of this by one of the Jockey Ckib members, who said he was present.

When I left Brightoh, I went to York races, where Mr. Cookson took me off his horse Sir Harry, signifying I rode him booty.

I did my utmost to win this race with Sir Harry, and had the same desire of winning this race as ever I had to win on any horse I ever rode.

I must momit horses as they are. The affidr of Mr. Cookson, I see, is, like these others, of too much consequence to me not to particularize the circumstances, which are as follow:

Mr. Cookson saw me in York on the Sunday before the race, and he said, "Chifney, you will ride for me the week." When upon the exercise-ground, Mr. Cookson asked me if I thought Sir Harry's running the two miles for the Oatlands would would hurt him for his next day's race. I told Mr. Cookson that in Sir Harry's situation I thought he would run better the second day from his running the first; upon which Mr. Cookson said;, "He shall run;" and it being a handicap.

Sir Harry was five years old, carried 8st. 7lb.

Wonder was six years old, carried Sst.

Cockfighter was four years old, carried 7st. 7lb. Cockfighter w on, and Wonder second. Sir Harry last. After the race, I told Mr. Cookson that Sir Harry was slow, and not able to run, and that I wished him to back Cockfighter to win on the next day, notwithstanding his having to carry even weights with Sir Harry.

Mr. Cookson then ordered me to attend him on the next morning. On this same afternoon Mr. Cookson called at the stables to see Sir Harry; and seeing me near the stable, he called me into the stable, by the side of him and his groom, and questioned me about Sir Harry's running, and made several excuses for Sir Harry's not running better. I thought Mr, Cookson and his groom, who was more fit for a tap-boy than a training-groom, were making out that I had rode Sir Harry a cheat. It was Sir Harry's condition that made him run so indifferently.

When Mr. Cookson was going to his carriage, I begged him not to let any person talk him out of what I had said to him, that Sir Harry could not run, and for him by no means to think of backing him.

On the following morning I waited upon Mr. Cookson, and he was getting more inclined to think Sir Harry would win, and continued making excuses for Sir Harry's running on the day before. I repeated to him not to think about his winning.

Mr. Cookson said Cockfighter did not run, neither did Wonder. He then said Sir Harry must win to-day, as those were post-horses he had to run against. I said 1 did not know about the horses he had to run against, but I did know that Sir Harry could not run, and I felt it my duty to tell tell him In that forcible manner. Mr. Cookson said, "Very right."

I then told Mr. Cookson that they said I had rode Sir Harry a cheat, and that I had been told it in two places. Mr. Cookson acknowledged they did say'so. I left Mr. Cookson. After this his groom came to me, to tell me that Mr. Cookson wished for another person to ride Sir Harry.

After this I was in the room at the Dring-houses, with Mr. Tyziman, one of the grooms, and others, and Tyziman said, "Chifney, our " north-country-gentlemen do not like your way " of riding Sir Harry; and they say they will not " have such sort of riding here." I thought it most proper to say but little to Tyziman, as it would guide his betting, but to wait to let Sir Harry's running answer for me. I then went upon the course to see them run; and when in the betting-stand, and when Sir Harry was running, Mr, Cookson asked mc if I had betted upon the race; I said, "Yes, Sir, I have betted thirty " to twenty, with Mr. Cholmondeley, Sir Harry " is beat. I wish Cockfighter had run, as that " would have made it safe." But it turned out safe. There were four of those post-horses, as Mr. Cookson called them, started against Sir Harry, and Sir Harry was last.

After this Mr. Cookson came to me in the standing-house, and said, "Chifney, you was ' very right about Sir Harry." I told Mr. Cookson that I had nearly been sacrificed several times for these last twenty years, and all from the noblemen and gentlemen falling dupes to those cripples who have neither knowledge or honesty.

In my own defence I was drove to tell my knowledge of horses' condition, and the effects of it, which was my great advantage upon the turf. I believe I was the cause of winning two of the greatest races through it that ever were run, theoatlands at Ascot in 179I, and the Oatlands at Newmarket in 1792, I mcan where more money was depending.

122 On the evening before running, I took the liberty of asking Mr. Vauxhall CLirk to tell Mr. Bullock, I thought he might lose the Oatlands from his not thinking as I did, that his horse Toby could win; Mr. Clarke told me Mr. Bullock and his people backed his other horse Buzzard, which I thought made him not take pains to get a person to ride Toby that was in high practice in riding, as the person engaged was not so; and that I would give one hundred guineas could I ride Toby, But I did not know if it would be proper that I should ride him, from the insult His Royal Highness so lately received at Newmarket. And I begged for Mr. Bullock to persevere in trying to have Lord Clermont's rider as Buzzard had no chance whatever of winning; and that Toby, I thought, had no chance of being beat, without it was by riding. " Mr. " Bullock (1

said) may think me impertinent pre-" tending to know his horses better than he does himself; but 'tis so, and a few hours will shew " it."

Mr. Bullock had Lord Clermont's rider to ride Toby, and Toby won. Buzzard was beat a great way by several horses. Toby became a great favourite before starting, and the odds got high against Buzzard. I won eleven hundred guineas on Toby this race. Mr. Cauty betted me seven hundred to forty-nine, and four hundred to twenty-four. There were fifty-six nominations at one hundred guineas eacli in this race; and twenty picked horses started, I see it as a necessity to name this meritorious-ness, by way of proof against any more of those bad constructions that might have lurked in some minds, to say that Chifney's was imposture, where he said to the Prince of Wales, on the 20th of October 179? why Escape was beat, and why he thought Escape would win on the following day. Seen in page 75.

This sort of apologizing of mine for the good horse Escape, I saw was to the field greek. Had I not been forced in my own defence, I would not at those times liave named about the condition of horses, and the effects of it, to any person for one thousand guineas.

Before I mentioned to His Royal Highness that I wished to have my orders to ride from any other person than Mr. W. Lake, I had wished His Royal Highness to discharge all his people that belonged to his race-horse stable.

I was informed the Duke of Bedford found it difficult to match his horses without allowing weight for my riding them.

Another nobleman, a great acquaintance of the Duke of Bedford's, and who is now a member of the Jockey Club, told me that he had such a high opinion of my riding, that he had made up his mind a long time back never to make a match where I had to ride against him. I told his lordship, that he, or the Jockey Club, ought to give me three hundred guineas a year, for, because I was thought to ride better than others, I found I was not to be used.

When

When the Prince left the turf on account of Escape's running, that renowned sportsman, Mr. Richard Vernon, said, that " the Prince had the best horses, and the best jockey; he was best " off the turf."

In 1802, at Brighton and Lewes race time, as the Prince of Wales was walking on the Steyne, holding a gentleman's arm, I told His Royal Highness, that they cried out very much for him at Newmarket. His Royal Highness said, "Sam Chifney, there's never been a proper apology " made; they used me and you very ill. They " are bad peoplepll not set foot on the ground " more." I was delighted with His Royal High-ness's answer, but at the same time I think it a very great hardship on Newmarket tradespeople to suffer from those above mentioned characters, bad in tongues, offending the Prince and his friends so that they will not come to Newmarket.

It appeared to me, that Sir Charles Bunbury was, in a manner, the only steward that acted.

That

That this business most likely was left chiefly, or quite to Sir Charles's management. And after my having gone through the examination above mentioned, every unprejudiced man must have been well satisfied that my conduct on riding Escape did not appear improper, than from the very great part that Sir Charles had chose to take in seconding those abuses on my riding Escape. And knowing those abuses were gone abroad, and such a very particular occasion as this, it certainly was Sir Charles Bunbury's duty to the Jockey Club, c. to have given their clerk orders to inform the public, that the Jockey Club had been imposed upon for a short time, concerning Chifney's riding His Royal Highness the Prince of Wales's horse Escape, unfiiir; and that the Prince of Wales and the Jockey Club had taken every pains to make themselves perfectly satisfied, that it was a false, malicious representation. Had this been done, it would have done away those characters from libelling the Prince 127 and me for these twelve years to the vvorkl, running Escape a cheat. Sir Charles Bunbury's stewardship to the Jockey Club was very singular in other respects, A (ew years back that one of the persons was sent to prison for breaking into a nobleman's stable to poison a liorse for his race. Sir Charles Bunbury's groom named it about at Newmarket, that his master, Sir Charles Bun-bury, had told him, that he dare not search too far into this business concerning those persons breaking into the stable to poison a horse for his race, as he was afraid there were too many in the Jockey Club that knew too much about it.

Noblemen and gentlemen might bet from those characters with no motives whatever but thinking they were backing a person of very superior judgment.

Mr. E. X. Tumor's horse, Oscar, run at Newmarket on the 17th and 18th of October 1798, and the first of those races was as rascally a race on Oscar's side, as horse can be made to run.

This

Tliis was very visible to sportsmen that were then on the turf those two clays. Why did not Sir Charles Banbury strike this character off from being used by any members of the Jockey Club? but instead of this being done, those characters that are supposed to have to do with those breaking into stables to poison horses for their race, and that trained Oscar for the abovementioned rascally race; those characters has and have, with Colonel Leigh's assistance, worked themselves into the management of the Prince of Wales's race horses, c. and worked me out of His Royal Highness's service.

I received a letter, dated the 7 th November 1803, for me to be discharged from the Prince's service, and my pension to cease to this date, for my ingratitude to His Royal Highness, and my son William's atrocious conduct to Colonel Leigh. Where my ingratitude has been to the Prince I know not. My pension I sold.

I could get no redress from the Prince, nor by lavv.

129 law, (for I have tried both,) against the bad usage myself and children met with from Colonel Leigh, Equerry to the Prince. I have desired my children, from their cradle, not to tell a lie, as they can never untcll it; never to be aggressors, to taunt or offend in any way, but endeavour to make themselves respected, by acting to all in; i becoming, dutiful manner; but to let no difficulties make them tell an untruth, as that unmans them; and for them to use vengeance, so far as they are able, against insulting injuries.

The conduct of Colonel Leigh toward my son William was an atrocious aggression, by representing him to a gentleman of the turf, on the 28th of April, as the greatest rogue and rascal living. This not only hurt the boy's feelings, but may be the means of depriving him of his livelihood.

Colonel Leigh did the same to his brother Samuel, and turned him out of stable and house from board, and would not pay him any thing for riding races on the Prince's horses three years. R He

He and bis brother William badbut eigbt guineas a-jear wage?, the same as the least boy in the stable, for which he rode exercise the same as the other boys. His riding the Prince's races was an extra expense to the boy, in clothes, c. They had given-Colonel Leigh, nor others, no offence, and I have reason to believe they were both dutiful and valuable servants.

Colonel Leigh also imposed upon their sister. He ordered her up, in the Prince's name, servant to Carl ton-House, (I have the letter,) to be under the direction of Mrs. Willis the housekeeper. After having been there turned of three years, and her age turned twenty-two, and no wages alloucd her, and from Colonel Leigh's telling me, in the presence of Mr. Sandi-ver of Nev, market, that the Prince had never ordered the girl to Carlton-House, or any thing about her, and from Colonel Leigh's bad usage of me and my two sons, I ordered the girl to leave Carlton-House.

On the 31st of May 1803 I was credibly in- iprmed formed Colonel Leigh had represented me to the Prince to be the worst fellow living.

And in those last October Meetings, as my son was standing by me on the exercise-ground, Colonel Leigh, the Prince's Equerry, rode, calling to Mr. Christopher Wilson, one of the Stewards of the Jockey Club, to give Sam Chifney his stick to lick me with. Mr. Wilson was on foot, with a stout stick in his hand, with another gentleman on foot with him. Colonel Leigh was at me the same again to a gentleman on the race-ground; and he knew I had been ill for two years, from losing the use of my limbs.

My son William knowing of those and other insulting, injurious usage of Colonel Leigh to me, himself, and his brother, and knowing also that I could get no redress from the Prince, nor by law, the boy licked Colonel Leigh. This is my son William's atrocious conduct to Colonel Leigh, for which Colonel Leigh is about to punish him in a court of justice; while myself and family are unable to obtain redress for undeserving insults and R 2 injuries.

injuries. I would rather see myself and boys starved to death than their hands should be tied against such usage; it is destroying courage, which cherishes badness, and those who would be good become civil rogues.

From Mr. W. Lake's and Neale's conduct, (pages 86 and 90), Sir Charles there want determined up to his office; but after my examination finished, (page 99,) what Sir Charles's motives were for renewing it again to the Prince (page 112), I know not. (Page 127) Sir Charles might then speak from rumour or appearance, in seeing some led in their betting by persons that are reported to have been concerned with others that broke into a stable to poison a horse for his race. Lord Sackville, Mr. Delme Ratcliffe, and Colonel Leigh, the Prince's Equerry, have for many years been led in their betting by those suspected of bflno; connected with stable-breakers. I left Lord Sackville for this reason, telling his Lordship the same, and my authorwhich was, that Bloss and Casborne were up all night, riding about, from their their being alarmed at a person called Old Tight being taken to justice for breaking into a stable to poison a horse for his match of five hundred guineas; and this Bloss his Lordship engaged to be under me in my training.

In 1794 Frank More was training-groom to Lord Sackville, and this More I saw was too much acquainted, for me, with Richard Goodi-son, then training-groom at Newmarket; therefore I made up my mind to have nothing to do with Lord Sackville's race-horses, if More was not discharged; and he was discharged, as I thought. After this it came out that Frank More, c. c. were colleagues of Casborne and Old Tight in breaking into a stable to poison a horse for his race, and in what is called pigeoning, at the time of the drawing of the Irish Lottery.

When I told this to Mr. Delme, (meaning Mr. Delme Ratcliffe,) and my author, that he had- it from Old Tight, Mr. Delme's answer was, "Why " it can't be so, Chifney! and he don't like to " change his nurse, I see!"

When

When I told Colonel Leigh that this said Bloss and Prank More were improper characters for him to employ in training the Prince's horses, I got myself much insulted. In 1800, when at Lewes I was going to ride the Prince's horse Knowsley for the Ladies' Plate, and just before saddling, that I attended on for my orders how to ride, this Bloss and Frank More were instantly called for aloud amongst the gentlemen and bettors, to give orders how I was to ride Knowsley. Directly on seeing I was to have orders from such characters, my brow came nearly over my eyes. It required a great general to give perfect orders for Knowsley in this race; to know both horses' fortes, the course they were going to run, each horse's condition, what they were best able to bear, and how Knowsley was to be sailed on all variety of changes that might occur in running. The mare, his greatest antagonist, had a bent sinew on her fore leg, and not well to run, and Knowsley was not within twenty-one pounds of his best form of running. Bloss and

Frank

Frank More were lost to their fortes and condition, and riding they know little more of than seeing horses run with their riders on their backs; but an errand of their orders I should take care to polish in my riding, which I did. I could have won on Knowsley more than four lengths. I could have won this same race on the mare more than six lengths.

As for Neale's improper conduct, in objecting me to the Prince's service, c. I look upon Neale as a dupe to more artful scoundrels than himself; for he appears to me as ready to hark rudely, from the clacks of others, as a cur is to bark at the clap of hands.

From Sir Charles's being imposed upon twice on the affair of Escape, I think it made him timorous in acting up to his office, to search into this gang that impose upon a field of noblemen and gentlemen who run horses for sport for themselves and the nation upon the most noble and honourable motives. Those characters can give much information, tell more than they ought to know, and more than they do know. There's mostly a knowing one or two that is hungry and likes to be fed by those improper characters, and then intrude themselves on noblemen and gentlemen in giving great praises to those that will tell them the most about their masters' and other horses. The training-grooms want a new lesson at Newmarket; that is, not to be other people's servants in telling horses, but let their masters tell their own horses by their betting, c.

I think no man more ready than Sir Ciiarles Bunbury to clear bad ones away; but he must, like all good men in office, be well seconded.

Before I sold my pension, I asked Colonel Leigh to be pleased to ask His Highness's leave for me to sell my pension, as I wanted it towards paying my debts. Colonel Leigh told me His Royal Highness said he was glad for me to sell it. I then wished to have a few words in writing from His Royal Highness, as I could then sooner sell it, and get a better price for it. Colonel Leigh and Mr. Caskoin told me I could not have it, c. I then then named those particulars to Colonel OKelly and Counsellor Const. A gentleman in the Temple of the name of Taylor purchased it of me as I believe, at a fair price, on the same terms as I had it, viz. on the Prince's honour.

In justice to the public and my children, and for my own satisfaction, I subjoin to the above statement the following

AFFIDAVIT,

Middlesex. Samuel Chifriey, of New- market in the county of Cam- bridge, rider, maketk oath and saith. That he this de-" ponent did ride a horse called Escapey hclo7iging to His Royal Highness the Prince of Walesy in a race in which he was beaten, on the twentieth day of October one thousand " seven hundred and ninety- one, at Newmarket; and that he a did did also at Newmarket ride the same horse in another race, on the next day, viz. the twenty-first day of OHober one thousand seven hundred- and ninety-one, in which he won. Andtliis doionent fur- ther saitji, That he made no hat ivhatsoever against Escape for the tw ntieth day of Octo- h(r one tjiousand seven hun- dred and ninety-one, when he was beatjn; but this depo- nent had one bet of twenty guineas ujion Escape and no ' more, for tjie twenty first day of October one thousand seven hundred and ninety-one, when he won; whicli was betted for the deponent by Mr. Vauxhall " Clark. And this deponentfar-" titer saith, That he was not " interested or concerned directly or indirectly in any other het what SOP ver against or for Es- cape for either of the before-" mentioned days. And this de-" lonent further majceth oath and saith, That previous to and on the said twentieth day of October one thousand seven hundred and ninetyone he " neither did nor caused, or pro-" cured to be done anything to check, hinder or irevrnt the said horse called Escape from winning, but on the contrary " that this deponent did every thing which his judgment sug-" gested to him, and his powers enabled him to make Escaps win the race he ran on the said twentieth day of October one thousand seven lamdied and ninety-one. And this dejio- nent farther maketh oath and s 2 saith,

"saithy TJuit ill no place that " lie has had the honour of " Vwing in since one thousand seven hundred and eigjity- foury that lie has not won a. guinea against any horse that was beat where that he either trained or rode him. And this " deponent further juajceth oath and saith, That that which " is asserted in the foregoing " narrative or statement is true, with his thoughts on the sam

SAMUEL CHIFNEY;

"Sworn before me this thirteenth day of March one thousand eight hundred and one,

John Collick."

TO THOSE
Who are not so well acquainted with
THE TURF.

And as it often happens that horses make changes in their twice running, I will mention a few of those changes.

The most extraordinary changes in horses running twice that I remember were with the Prince of Wales's horses Magpie, at Newmarket, and Traveller, at York. Magpie run at Newmarket on the Monday in the July Meeting JQO, two miles against Seagull; and Seagull beat him so easy that he had only to canter for more than the last last iialf mile to beat Magpie one liundred yards. Two elear days after, I rode Magpie, which was the first time of my riding him, and he won; and I think Magpie beat in this race a better runner than Seagull. I think Coriander was a better runner. Magpie beat in this race Schoolboy, Grey Diomed, Coriander, Skylark, c. Seagull, Magpie, Coriander, and Skylark were all of one age, and carried even weights in both races. Magpie, in his first race, carried 8st. 2lb. and in his second race 8st. and both races two miles. I heard no nuirmuring from any person about this extraordinary change; but from others' disappointments in their horses not winning this race, it pulled from theirmouthsgreat encomiums upon Chifney's riding. A gentleman came out of the crowd to me as I had just come from scale, and told me that Mr. Clarke was lamenting about his horse Schoolboy not winning the race, saying,, how unfortunate he was that the race had not been a. day sooner as then Chifney would not have rode 143 rode the Prince's horse, and there was no other person but him could ride, and that he won all his races this way; and, what was more extraordinary, no person knows how he wins them but himself. This gentleman then said, that the Duke of Bedford appeared much dissatisfied, thinking his horse Grey Diomed might have won this said race; and that His Grace said they had got his rider from him (meaning Chifiicy); and that he did not think of losing hhn, as helneant to have had (lim.

It may be proper for me to say a few words here on this subject. I had offered myself as rider to His Grace the Duke of Bedford, and was open to his Grace's service, from Epsom race till the day before this race, at two hundred guineas a year for life. My not agreeing to the Duke's terms, His Grace used another rider. I then was engaged, as I thought, on the same terms to the Prince of Wales as I had offered myself to the Duke.

Mr. Dawson's Coriander made a great change for the better in his twice running, on the 9th and nth of April 1792.

Mr. Christopher Wilson's capital running horse Champion, at York, in 1800, was first beat easily, several lengths, by Rolla. A clear day after. Champion beat Rolla several lengths; the first race a mile and a half, second race two miles each race 8st. 2lbs. each. How is the field to know which horse made the change in this race? One horse changing for the worse will make it appear the other changed for the better, that the wrong side may be censured.

Sir Charles Bunbury's capital running horse Sorcerer, in October Meeting 1800, made a great change in his running. He was first beat a great A ay by an inferior horse; he afterwards run in capital stile, and won.

I rode, and won, on the Duke of Bedford's horse Grey Diomed, five years old, 8st. 7lbs. a match against the Prince of Wales's horse Bubble, 145 blcj six years old, 7st, two miles, for three hundred guineas. This was a very hard race.

I then rode and won on the Prince of Wales's horse Bubble, 8st. 13lbs. for a subscription weight for age, four miles, against the Duke of Bedford's horse Grey Diomed, 8st. 6lbs. I could win this race many lengths in the last two hundred yards. Those two races were in 1790; the horses on both sides, and for both races, were thouo-ht to be well; and both races were as honestly rode against me as man can ride.

Had I rode those horses, and the changes in their running been thus against me, it's likely that I should have been censured, if not sacrificed. I rode this last race in a large hack saddle, a new one, and the eye of the stirrup-iron broke, and fell in running the first cjuarter of a mile; but I was my weight with the bridle.

I have seen horses chanc-e in their runninp- on the same day, from their being brought out too full, that a man might be censured and sacrificed by taking him oft after a heat is run.

And a horse will change in his two days running very much for the worse if he has been fed and watered too plentifully. I have no doubt but that's the case at times, and from a supposed kindness to the horse, by unskilful people. A horse should be fed and watered lightly for his second day's race; for, from a horse being sharp set on the muzzle, and heated with running, his veins and bowels are empty, narrow, and dry; so that what is given him is likely to stay with him till after his second race; and if a horse happens to be thus overfilled, it must at times affect him very much in his second running. None but the person who had tlie management of Skylark knows but he might be thus sent out to run his second race with Escape. Skylark was a wonderful close and large-carcased horse, and started close to his stable this last day; and if thus overfed, he liad not so great a time as horses generally have have to walk to circulate his bowels. Though Escape was obliged to go over to the four-mile post for his starting, (and it must have tlie same effect upon horses as it has u)on riders, in i)ropor-tion to their species,) it often happens where a rider has been trained for riding, (and the manner is nearly the same as that adopted in training horses,) that a rider of so light a weight as seven stone at times will weigh seven pounds or more on the following day. By this it may be conceived how a horse at times may be affected if too kindly fed, c. for his second day's race; thus a rider's character is staked against the training-groom's management and conduct.

Some people say by Sir Charles Bunbury as they do by me, that Sir Charles at times runs his horses to lose intentionally, and this has been said of Sir Charles ever since his horse Bellario lost and won easy, at Newmarket, in 1770 down I don't think Sir Charles can know of those things being said of him.

148 to the year 1802; and of late, when those things have been mentioned in my hearing, I have told those people, that I believed neither myself or they ever saw Sir Charles Banbury run a horse but that he had the best intentions for the horse to win. The cant expression at Newmarket was, that Sir Charles said Bellario had the head-ache on the first day that he was beaten. But Sir Charles Bunbury and others well know, by their own stables, that Chifney gave them a good drilling in 1791, in teaching them the knowledge of horses changing in their twice running. This not only tauo-ht the knowledge of horses' condition, and the effects of it, but it must prevent much dissatisfaction amongst noblemen and gentlemen in unfair censuring their servants in

horses changing in their running. I believe horses never run two days together alike; sometimes the difference is trifling, sometimes much.

In Spring Meeting 1791, Mr. W. Lake, Neale, and Bill Price drew up together on the race- race-ground, and called me to them, and signified to me that I had written an anonymous letter to the Prince, that Escape and Magpie were both to lose at Ascot in i790, as Hindley was to ride the in; and that they would all leave the Prince if there was not a change made. I told them I thought it very necessary there should be a change made. " I am not one of those envious, coward- ly rascals to stab thus at a person in the dark."

Mr. Lake and Neale told the Prince that I had lost His Highness's race on the IQth of October 1790. I had rode the Prince's horse Fitzwilliam for a Stakes, thirteen subscribers, one hundred guineas each, and was beat by Lord Grosvenor's horse Rhadamanthus. It was as much as Rha-damanthus could do just to beat him; and directly the race was over, that 1 was walking back to scale, his Royal Highness said, "Sam Chif-" ney, Mr. Lake and Frank Neale say you have lost this race by riding." I then wished His Royal Highness not to let any thing induce him to match till I saw His Royal Highness when I came from scale. Directly I came from the scale, His Koyal Highness said Mr. Lake and PVank Ncale had hccn at him again that I had lost the race. I directly made answer, "Your Royal Highness, Rhacuimanthus has now no " engagements upon him, and upon such an oc " casion as this I am sure Lord Grosvenor will oblige your Highness with the horse, and I ". pray your Royal Highness let them be " matched; and for Rhadamanthus thus to give Fitzvvilliam twenty-one pounds to run the same course, and for me to ride Rhadamanthus; " and I wish your Royal Highness to bet five or " ten thousand upon Rhadamanthus, and it is a " thousand guineas to one shilling Rhadamanthus wins. I will then show them such riding as they never can be made to know."

When the Prince left the race-ground, he went on the other side of the town to see the horses exercise, and the Prince came riding down the hill from from his race-horses, and said Frank Neale had been telling him again that I had lost the race with Fitzwilliam. I told His Royal Highness that Neale was a weak man. It did not appear to me that theie was any offer made to have them matched. I did not feel myself satisfied, as the Prince seemed to be nettled about my being beat, from telling me so often about the same thing. As for Mr. Lake and Neale's saying and pretending that Fitzwilliam was able to beat Rhadaman-thus, why Rhadamanthus was rated to be one of the first runners of his years. It was three to one upon him against the field; and Fitzwilliam had been tried, a short time before the 8th of October, against Smoker and Chambooe, the same course these horses had been running, and Chambooe had beat Fitzwilliam an astonishing way. Chambooe was beat easily by Smoker, and Smoker was thought not so good a runner as Rhadamanthus. But it seemed as if Mr. Lake and Neale had lost sight of this trial. It must be

from from Fitzwilliam's winning on the Sth of October 1700. He then won a race of twelve hundred and fifty guineas, and he won it by two or three lengths, at even weights, though the horse he beat could have given him, in this race, if rode with judgment, 14 lb. and have beat him for certain. I had not mentioned this chance man–ner of Fitzwilliam's winning, as it would only serve to inform my opponents;

for what I mentioned to one I saw generally served the field. Where I acted out of the usual ways, both in riding and training, I was continually abused where I got beat; and those trainers that abused my training were all glad to follow my ways, so far as they are able to make them out. I have trained but seldom.

The Duke of Bedford took me off his horses tvice, and threatened me a third time. The first time of my having the honour to ride for the Duke of Bedford was his horse Fidget, for the Claret Stakes at Newmarket, on the 27th of

April

April 1787. Ontlie July following Goodison engaged me to ride the Duke of Queensberry's liorse Mulberry against Lord Clermont's Markho, and Mulberry was beat easily; and it appeared to me that Mulberry was not able to go a proper running pace In any part of this race; and when I came from scales, James Barton, Esq. told me that Goodison had been telling the gentlemen that I had rode Mulberry booty; and Mi-. Barton said he told him if he dared to say so agam he would ram his stick down his throat. Goodison had been at these sort of abuses, and others, to me, for a long time before this, that it made gentlemen afraid to employ me. This Goodison insulted me in public, that I rode Escape booty on the 20th of October 1791. I have reasons to believe this Goodison is the original cause of the Duke of Bedford and the Prince of Wales having been thus troubled and disturbed concerning me in my riding, by Goodison having been capable of imposing upon the public, reporting me to u ride ride booty, 8cc. that from his villainous conduct it continually kept others to assist in keeping the minds of the public ripe to think and say bad of me.

In the following October Meeting the Duke of Bedford took me off his horse Fidget, after riding him the first of his four five hundred-guinea matches against Lord Grosvenor's Meteor. This was on the Monday; and on the Friday follovi-ing, Mr. Tumor, a gentleman from Bexley in Kent, told me that the conversation at all the dinners that week had been about Fidget and Meteor's race, whether it was a hard race, an easy race, or whether Fidget was beat at all. This soon showed itself farther. The same night the Duke of Bedford told his groom, Mr. Matt Stephenson, to go to Chifney, and tell him that the Prince of Wales wished his jockey South to ride

The Duke's decease prevents me farther explaining what I had said to his Grace, after Fidget's first race with Meteor.

Fidget 155 Fidget his match against Meteor to-morrow; but tell Chifney " he is to ride for me as usual."

On the following day, (Saturday,) the first race that came on was Mr. OKelly's Augusta, 8st. and Lord Derby's Paul, Sst. 7lb. Ditch-in, for two hundred guineas. I rode Augusta, and she was beat. She had run Paul a hard and near race. Directly I came from the scale, I was told Goodison had much abused me for being beat on Augusta, and that he had matched her again to run the same day, and the same course, Augusta Sst. and Paul Sst. 4lb. for five hundred guineas. About this time Mr. OKelly came to me, and said he was very angry with himself at letting the fellow have the mare to run again.

I told Mr. OKelly as he had done it, I wished him not to bet upon her. Mr. OKelly said the fellow had asked him to stand fifty guineas with him on the match. I told Mr. OKelly to get it off, and let the fellow pay for his impudence. As Mr. OKelly was thus talking to me, the Duke u2 of 156 of Qiieensberry came up and said, "I don't know what it is that my man means. I thought " your niaie had the advantage in tlie race." I made answer, "It was as your Grace saw it."

After this, I was told that Goodison wanted Lord Derby to let him off the match; but his Lordship said he would not have those liberties taken with him, but that he might, if he liked, run as they had run before, for two hundred guineas.

Then came Fidget and Meteor's race, and a long distance from the winning-post Meteor chucked up his head against his rider, Mr. Piatt; and it v iis quite play for Meteor, as he run clear away from Fidget. As the horses were walking back to the scale, James Barton, Esq. and Lord Henry Fitzroy came up to me, and his Lordship said, ' Chifney, I give you joy at Meteor's beat- ing Fidget; for had Fidget beat Meteor, I believe you weald never have rode another " horse at Newmarket."

This

This speech of his Lordsliip was double joy to mecherishing good conduct is spurning at bad.

Then came on Augusta and Paul, and Paul had beat Augusta such a very great distance, more than hali a mile from home, that there was not a person scarce, that would take one hundred guineas to one on the race. Mr. Pratt rode Augusta, Sam Arnold rode Paul both his races.

The field are as lost to parts of the best riding as they are to training.

Some through craft have imposed upon the Prince. As I am well informed the Prince of Wales says, Chifney can't train, and has never used me for training; and I have nearly been the same sacrificed by the field being the same lost to some parts of the very best of riding.

Now in my own defence I will name one of those very fine parts in riding a race, as it is thrown in my face to this time as a very great fault in my riding, viz. my riding with a loose rein.

The Duke of Bedford was near taking me off his horses, saying, the people teased him because I rode his horses with a loose rein, and desired me to hold my horse fast in his running; I was sorry his grace was thus troubled, as it puts a horse's frame all wrong;- and his speed slackened where the horse has that sort of management to his mouth. My reins appeared loose, but my horse had only proper liberty, and mostly running in the best of attitudes. It's usual, when that grooms are talking and giving orders to their riders, to hold the horse fast in his running; and where a liorse is intended to make play, their orders mostly are, to hold the horse fast by the head and let him come, or come along with him; but it's very much against a horse to hold him fast, or let him bear on his rein in his running; it makes him run with his mouth more open, and pulls his head more in or up. This causes him at times, to run in a fretting, jumping attitude, with his fore legs more open; sometimes it causes him to run stag-necked; this makes the horse point his forelegs, (otherwise called straight legged.) Sometimes it makes the horse run with his head and neck more down, crowding and reaching against his rider. This reaching his neck against his rider, pulls the horse's forelegs out farther than the pace occasions. In all those attitudes his sinews are more worked and extended, he's more exertion, his wind more locked and thus reaching and pointing his fore-legs makes them dwell and tire.

That the first fine part in riding a race is to command your horse to run light in his jnouth; it keeps him the better together, his legs are the more under him, his sinews less extended, less exertion, his wind less locked; the horse running thus to order, feeling light for his rider's wants; his parts are more at ease and ready, and can run considerably faster when called upon, to what he can when that he has been running in the fretting, sprawling attitudes, titudes, with part of his rider's weight in his mouth.

And as the horse comes to his last extremity, finishing his race, he is the better forced and kept straight with manner, and fine touching to his mouth. In this situation the horse's mouth should be eased of the weight of his rein, if not, it stops him little or much. If a horse is a slug he should be forced with a manner up to this order of running, and particularly so if he has to make play, or he will run the slower, and jade the sooner for the want of it.

The phrase at Newmarket is, that you should pull your horse to ease him in his running When horses are in their great distress in run ning they cannot bear that visible manner of pulling as looked for by many of the sportsmen; he

The word " manner" is knowing, putting, keeping self and horse in the best of attitudes. This gives readiness, force, and quickness.

should i6i should be enticed to ease himself an inch a time as his situation will allow.

This should be done as if you had a silken rein as fine as a hair, and that you was afraid of breaking it.

This is the true way a horse should be held Jast in his running.

N. B. If the Jockey Club will be pleased to give me two hundred guineas, I will make them a bridle as I believe never was, and I believe can never be excelled for their light weights to hold their horses from running away, and to run to order in, as above mentioned, as near as I thus can teach; and it is much best for all horses to run in such; and ladies in particular should have such to ride and drive in, as they not only excel in holding horses from running away, but make horses step safer, ride pleasanter, and carriage handsomer.

I have said in page 144, horses change in their twice running. If a horse is in perfect fitness for running, he immediately hecomes exhausted, little or much; he must then change in his running. A horse cannot keep his perfect fitness for running more than one race, till rested. I X 2 have have seen one sweat between tlieir twice running change horses for the worse astonishingly. It is destruction to horses to sweat them in the manner they are sweated at Newmarket, as the practice there is to sweat them once in six days, sometimes oftener; and between those days of sweating, it is usual for the horse to go out twice a day, each time having strong exercise. In. these sweating days the horses are mostly covered with cloths, two or three times doubled, and go in their sweats six miles, more or less, and at times go tolerably fust. Directly the horse pulls uy, he is hurried into the stable which is on the spot for that purpose. As soon as he gets in, there is often more cloths thrown upon him, in addition to those he has been his sweat in. This is done to make the horse sweat the more, and he stands thus for a time, panting, before he is stripped for scraping; that with being thus worked clothed, and stoved, it so affects him at times, that he keeps breaking out iti fresh sweats, that it pours from him, when scraping, as if water liad been tin-own on him. Nature cannot bear this. The horses must dwindle.

I think, in the first place, that the horse has been too long at this sort of work for his sinews; then the clothing and stoving him forces his juices from him in such quantities, must destroy their spirits, strength and speed; and much clothing jades horses. A horse don't meet with this destruction when he runs, for then he is likely to be lighter in his carcase, lighter in his feet, having plates on, not shoes, which is wonderfully in favour of his sinews; and he is without clothes, and not stoved, and his course in running is very seldom dom more than four miles; therefore this difference in sweating and running is immense.

When a liorse pulls up from his running, he has time given him to move gently in the air, and usually scraped out upon the turf, and by these means the horse perspires no more than suits his nature.

When a horse is first taken into work after having had a long rest, his carcase is then large and

Horses should have different brakes against weather, to scrape in. Buildings for this, I think, would be most proper made after the horse-dealers' rides in London; open in front being out of the weather, and not out of the air. Places of this sort would be much the best for horses to saddle in; for horses saddling in those close, dark stables, they at times break out with great perspiration when saddlingj and in fine, roomy-places of this sort there would be proper room, c. for noblemen and gentlemen sportsmen to command a sight of the horses at saddling; and horses are less timid being in a crowd than they are to hear it and not see it.

heavy.

i67 heavy, and the practice is to put more clothes upon the horse, and order him to go a longer sweat. But the horse in this stage of his training is the less able to bear more cloths, and go further in his sweats; for the horse himself being heavy, that, with boy and cloths, at times has a great weight upon his legs; that with this pressure and his work heating him, it makes his sinews full and weak; and thus working a little too fast or too long upon his sinews at one stretch, they are forced out of their places. This once done, the horse seldom stands training after.

It is ignorant cruelty in the great number of horses being thus unskilfully lamed at Newmarket; and gentlemen not only lose the use of their horses and their money by it, but it so greatly deprives them of the sport that they otherwise would have.

168 The first fine care In training horses for running, and hunters and liacks for hard riding, Is, to train their legs to be able to carry their carcase; using them first to short exercise, short gallops, short sweats, and giving time between their work for their sinews to rest, or the best of legs will become destroyed.

Horses' legs are very soon destroyed at first coming into work; but when they have had time to be well trained, scarce any running or riding will hurt them.

Some few, I am Informed, have a way of pinching their race-horses in their meat and water. This is another certain way of perishing a horse in his spirits and strength. Where a horse is too large in his carcase, he should be well fed, as horses, I believe, for the most part of them are at Newmarket; and, instead of pinching him in his wiitcr, where a horse is greedy of it, he slionld be watered very often, and at all times as much as he will drink; he will then drink less, and come straight and strong in his carcase.

The outcry is. Why are there so few good runners, or that the turf-horses degenerate? Some say they think it is from running horses too young. My opinion is this; viz. That the best running mares are trained till their running is gone from them little or much, then turned into the stud exhausted of their juices, as above described. Perhaps drop a foal on the following year, and so on year after year, suckling one foal while breeding another. The mare is thus turned into the stud, drained of her strength, and her continually breeding keeps her so, without she Y lays 170 Jays herself barren a year or two by her mis-standing to the horse. This chance manner of her laying herself fallow gives her an opportunity of recovering her juices, or strength to enable her to breed a stronger foal, provided the horse that is to her is the same in proper plight.

And it is the same with the horses. They are turned out of training into the stud, thus drained of their nature; and the better runner he is, the more he is immediately pressed with iiumbeis of the best mares, and in a manner all to the stau lions at one time.

These are my reasons why the turf-horses degenerate in strength, speed, and beauty.

FINIS.

D. N. SHURY, PRINIKR, BERWICK STTxeET, ioHO, LONDON.

Webster Family Library of Veterinary Medicine Cummings School of Veterinary Medicine at Tufts University 200 Westboro Road Morth Grafton. MA 01535